HOW TO SAVE YOUR FOURTH MARRIAGE

One Person Can
Transform a Relationship

TERRI CROSBY

BALBOA.PRESS

A DIVISION OF HAY HOUSE

Balboa Press books may be ordered through booksellers or by contacting:

Balboa Press
A Division of Hay House
1663 Liberty Drive
Bloomington, IN 47403
www.balboapress.com
844-682-1282

Print information available on the last page.

ISBN: 978-1-9822-7835-9 (sc)
ISBN: 978-1-9822-7837-3 (hc)
ISBN: 978-1-9822-7836-6 (e)

Library of Congress Control Number: 2021925190

Balboa Press rev. date: 02/15/2022

CONTENTS

To Mother Nature, with all my heart.
I am forever yours.

Important Note to Readers

While I believe that most relationship challenges can be resolved more easily than we might imagine, this is not meant to encourage anyone anywhere at any time or for any reason to stay in a mentally, emotionally, or physically abusive situation. Don't think twice. Do what it takes to get out safely.

If you're confused about whether to leave, call on a levelheaded friend, counselor, or trusted health professional for a reality check. Have them help you make a plan for yourself, one that provides for your safety and well-being.

GLOSSARY OF TERMS

save (your marriage): Realize the truth about it. To save your marriage, save you. Live by the truth of who you are.

match: A person or thing able to contend with another as an equal in quality or strength. In partnerships, a match between two people creates a balanced cycle of relating, whether the relating is pleasant or difficult.

true-you: The you that expresses your Inner Being. True-you is divine (spirit) and human (flesh) as one—your godself.

not-you/false-you: The counterfeit version of you. Not-you is the adjusted version that helped you fit in. Not-you is who you think you are. It is the person you learned to be, felt obligated to be, or were forced to be.

Inner Being: The higher intelligence lifestream called "you." Sometimes referred to as your Higher Self, it gives Inner Guidance toward true-you.

Inner Guidance: The counsel offered by your Inner Being through nudges, urges, random thoughts, dreams, emotions, and inspiration. Inner Guidance gives us the ability to understand something without the need for conscious reasoning.

Survival Self/CaveMan/CaveWoman: The part of our human composition concerned with survival and reproduction.

The Five Core Skills for Making Changes: breathe, receive, observe, reflect, rehearse. We use the first four core skills (breathe, receive, observe, reflect) to light up true-us. The fifth skill (rehearse) supports and reinforces what is found.

breathe: The first core skill. Breathing is a unique skill because it is both voluntary and involuntary. We voluntarily take air into the lungs and then expel it—take a deep breath to calm ourselves, for instance. We're also being breathed while we sleep. If Source is breathing us, then Source's wisdom also comes in on our breath. To give attention to this wisdom—to grow our willingness to sense it and use it—takes a lifetime.

receive: The second core skill. To receive is to welcome what is. To be present and accept. When it rains, let it rain.

observe: The third core skill. To observe is to step back from ourselves and examine what we said or did in a lighthearted, curious way, as if viewing someone else.

reflect: The fourth core skill. To reflect is to realize and harvest benefit from an experience, even if the experience was negative.

rehearse: The fifth core skill. Rehearsal is the practice of something. This can be intentional practice, or it can be unintentional (automatic). With intentional rehearsal, we do our best, adjust, and then do it over. Unintentional rehearsal is our automatic practice of behaviors, thoughts, and patterns that become our identity and personality.

Willie Daly, Irish matchmaker for fifty years:
"I still believe in marriage," he says with a chuckle.
"And I think everyone should marry as many times as they can."

ABOUT THE BOOK

The thought of a fourth failed marriage sent me to my knees. Why was I unable to keep an intimate relationship happily on track? Was something wrong with me? My failures, as I saw them, were personally difficult and professionally embarrassing. Either I was a relationship coach with bad luck and should be excused from the team, or I hadn't yet learned what made marriage work. Turns out it was the latter.

How to Save Your Fourth Marriage is what I did—I saved my fourth—which could be considered a miraculous accomplishment, given that 93 percent of fourth marriages end in divorce within five years.[1] Marriage might be one of the few activities we engage in where, for many of us, the more often we practice it, the worse our chances of success.

Whether you're having difficulty in your first relationship, or you're heading into marriage number eight, the information here is for you. It's not so much about how many times you've tried, but rather, do you want your relationship to work or work better? Do you wish to be happier together? If you love each other and don't know how to get along or how to become closer, this information is especially for you. Even if you've given it your best shot and have thrown your hands up, there is still hope.

There is hope because the quality of your relationship with your partner lives within *you*. The facets of how *you* relate to *you* are reflected by those whom you call partner, ex-partner, friend, enemy, and family. The way you treat others represents the way you treat yourself. The relationship you have with others *is* the relationship you have with yourself.

If you have an intimate relationship you believe is worth reviving, look no further than your own heart and mind. You'll save years of frustration and circling back if you can love yourself enough to change. You're the one—the only one—who can transform your life. By transforming yourself. You hold the magic wand. You can free yourself to be the person you are. When you liberate yourself to become *true-you*, this invites people around you to respond more freely as well—to be *true-them*.

How This Book Is Shared with You

I've done my best to make this information easy to absorb, with stories, bullet points, and suggestions. There are also dialogues with clients, using the names Her, Him, and Me. These consulting sessions show how issues are multilayered, how a seemingly small trouble spot, when unraveled, gives way to substantial understanding. You'll track how new possibilities begin to make sense to a client, and to yourself, too, as you read. I'm thankful for the generous men and women who have allowed me to write conversations based on those I had with them, so that I could offer them to you.

Although my fourth husband, Eric, passed away in 2017 from cancer, you'll get to know him and the journey we traveled together through shared stories and examples. Transforming my relationship with Eric taught me that it was possible to shift even the most stuck or awful circumstances by changing patterns that had been mine for a long time. I would not have believed this sort of thing possible had I not experienced it myself. Finding a deeper and more satisfying relationship with Eric was a miracle from every angle.

~~~~~

There are a hundred paths through the world
that are easier than loving. But who wants easier?
—Mary Oliver

They slipped briskly
into an intimacy
from which
they never recovered.

—F. Scott Fitzgerald

PART ONE

Does Anyone Need Fixing?

PART ONE

1

If at First...

EACH OF MY marriages began with hope and dedication, and a firm knowing that my partner would be the one I'd cherish forever. We would grow together. We'd fall more deeply in love over the years and hold hands into the golden sunset. My belief each time was that *this* marriage would be *the one.*

Faces and places certainly changed, but I was the common denominator. My marriages perfectly mirrored me and my patterns. Each marriage began as a happy-go-lucky summer breeze and then sometime between three and five years later, the icy north wind blew in. My fourth marriage followed the predictable pattern. In the beginning, Eric and I were carefree and relaxed—truly happy. We delighted in each other's company and laughed easily and often. We found agreement in all the right places. Communication was simple and inspiring. Sex was wonderful, the best I'd ever had. Eric seemed to know my body. He could somehow sense what pleased me physically, no instructions needed, which was a new experience.

But time passed, and by year three our joy had faded. By year four it had practically disappeared. What I noticed most was that Eric had become a weak version of himself. He was less adventurous, less of a risk taker, less bold. Instead of showing him compassion, I was annoyed that he'd gone soft and no longer carried himself with confidence. He deferred to my decision-making, seemed depressed, and drifted from one day to the next. Even so, I plodded on, hopeful that things would change. Maybe we would find our happy little bluebird place again.

One weekend morning, I opened my eyes to a lovely Sunday in Southern California, cheerfully anticipating the usual chat with Eric over coffee. No disagreement hung in the air. Nothing was wrong (that I could detect) as I wandered contentedly toward the kitchen to prepare a breakfast tray. But upon my return Eric was slumped against the bed pillows, looking defeated. I wondered if a bad genie had slipped into the bedroom while the coffee was brewing, decked Eric, and messed with his mind. It had been a surprise attack, and Eric lost the fight. Instead of being curious or open, I braced myself for the conversation. Worry engulfed me in those seconds standing there, coffee in hand, in our bedroom. There was a wide river of fear running through me.

When I asked Eric what was going on, he gave me one sentence. "Are you done with me yet?"

The question shocked me. I nearly dropped the coffee. No man had ever said that to me. At that moment I didn't care if my relationship with Eric was even worth saving. The prospect of losing another marriage flooded me with shame and frustration. How could I face one more divorce? How would I answer the inevitable questions, the unspoken judgments from friends and family, or the need to explain to the next possible partner about my four divorces? If Eric and I split up, would it be possible to summon enough faith in myself to counsel others about getting along?

It didn't occur to me that my reasons for wanting to rescue our marriage were not high-minded. I didn't pause to comprehend that my reaction was coming from fear, not love, or that my concern was not about Eric at that moment but about relieving myself of awful feelings. My desperation was simple. Eric seemed depressed and defeated, which meant failure. Again.

From my side of the bed, I handed Eric his coffee. He looked up at me, one arm propping his head. How would we gather up our last bits of relationship? Was there anything left to save? Maybe we were fine, or at least fine enough to get by. Maybe we could stagger through to a miracle and find the lucky pot of gold at the end of the rainbow. Maybe the only sensible thing to do was what I'd done many times before: take the hit, cut my losses, and start fresh.

I climbed into bed, arranged the pillows around me for a lengthy conversation, and pleaded, "Eric, please don't go anywhere. This is fixable. Give me a chance, and if nothing changes, we can call it quits." I don't remember caring whether he agreed or not.

At some point during our talk, however, something shifted. My belief in blame vanished. I don't recall the moment it happened. Nor do I understand why or even how. It wasn't until weeks later that it occurred to me: pointing the finger at him (or me) had lost its appeal that morning. This was a radical departure and a shining moment. This was a new sun, and it was rising.

What did resemble my past experiences was that my connection with Eric had run its course. Our Sunday morning reminded me of a scene from a war film where someone is running from an explosion in slow motion, with fire everywhere and debris flying. The dramatic soundtrack swells as metal moves through the air in an oddly beautiful way. My marriage had detonated and was up in flames. The shrapnel of impatience, panic, and fear swirled through the air—a live, moving sculpture of a life in review.

To go back to the drawing board of my life without a shred of evidence that the attempt would be successful wasn't a conscious decision—more like a swarm of questions. Was relationship resuscitation feasible at this late stage? Was it possible to personally pivot enough to change things for the better? What would that mean exactly? What would it require? Could I change, not just for the sake of rescuing our connection with each other but in a way that was authentic for me? Could the intimacy and harmony that I so desperately desired with him return? Underneath it all, could I become a different person than I thought I was?

Physician, Heal Thyself

To work things out with Eric, I took time off from being a relationship consultant and joined a closet company as a designer. After I shared my relationship woes with a trusted coworker, she recommended a relationship seminar, and I resolved to go with two of my friends, but they were no-shows. Thankfully, the speaker was knowledgeable and captivated the room with warmth and skill. She was funny and told compelling stories. Her women-only presentation centered around navigating male-female differences, which was of great interest to me since an ex-husband and I had created and taught a course entitled "Men's and Women's Reality."

As the seminar concluded, a tsunami of regret rolled over me for having lived so long without understanding what I had perceived about myself that evening. It confused me that the rest of the women in the room seemed happy and spoke to one another animatedly as they registered for upcoming events. Had these women missed the weight of the ideas presented? Why were they so chatty while I swam in grief? I was grateful that the two girlfriends I'd invited had bailed, leaving time for me to weep openly in my seat without discussion or explanation.

At last I headed to the front of the room to connect with the seminar leader. She was also the founder of the organization and she knew about my Men's and Women's Reality work. We talked about her research and how she had spoken to some of our students. Her husband had taken one of our classes. That was a full-circle moment for me.

In the weeks that followed, self-help CDs and audiobooks helped pass the hours spent behind the wheel in Southern California traffic for my job with the closet company. One day, overcome by new information, I pulled into a parking spot near a Santa Monica bagel shop. There I sat, my head in my hands and elbows on the steering wheel, listening intently to information from another thought leader that blew my mind. Inner tectonic plates of frustration grated across one another. Ancient glaciers of understanding collided inside me. Old beliefs were pulverized as new hunks of understanding heaved themselves into position. It was loud in there.

Eric's love for me was strong enough for him to stay around during my massive personal overhaul. However, he didn't take classes or seek outside assistance along with me. He read not a single book on personal growth or relationships. It never occurred to me to care whether he read anything, because my attention was on my own behavior. My focus was on finding reasons to believe I could become a person who could love myself, love men, and live happily with one for many years to come.

Slow Dance with Change

Thus far I had reasoned that if I had a problem with a husband, he probably needed a little fixing. If husband number one could be faithful, or husband number two could recognize and support who I am (instead of ask me to be different), or if husband number three could actually change (and not just talk about it), then the problems between us would magically vanish. Until things went south with number four—Eric—the idea of full responsibility had never found a home in me. It would have required a lot of work on my part and been far too humbling. My desire for change meant "Things around me should change. My husband should stop saying this or start doing that. I'm okay with myself, but let's tweak him."

My new commitment to self-examination pushed me to look within. What I discovered was a considerable stash of defense methods. My emotional or mental fists went up—often! Slowly, conscious efforts to inquire instead of accuse, to disarm instead of defend, to be curious instead of critical, paid off. As my fists went down, I asked more questions and made fewer assumptions. I learned to listen.

Here's the ugly-cry part. When I didn't defend myself or blame Eric, my own pain became obvious. Without attention on reasons to disapprove of his political beliefs, his career struggles, or his over-the-top messy office and pro music gear repair shop which spilled into the beautiful spaces of our home, my issues showed up front and center, and they were uncomfortable. That's why we avoid them, possibly for years. My pain was not enjoyable. You may not like yours, either, or the fact that one's pain platter comes with sides of sadness, grief, and humble pie. But if you're willing to address what causes the discomfort, the rewards are worth it.

At first addressing my personal issues seemed impossible and unwieldy. After all, where does one start? Perhaps we begin as the twig-like insect—the wood stick—approaching the giant redwood. The wood stick simply climbs. But we humans contemplate the worthiness of a climb, the effort required, and the possible payoff. We figure that climbing is probably a good thing if we can manage to find the will, stamina, and focus to stay on track instead of reverting to familiar strategies. In the past, when things got messy, I'd Houdini my way out of one circumstance and into another bright and shiny possibility. When the going got tough, I'd leave. I'd date or marry a new man.

But during that come-to-Jesus Sunday morning with Eric, standing still for a change was big. I didn't run. I took a look at myself and my views about the man in my bed, on my arm, in my life. That morning it occurred to me that my thoughts about him might have less to do with the truth of him and more to do with the truth of me and how I related to him.

Five Beliefs that Changed

During my first three marriages, my beliefs about relationships could be considered normal thinking.

> **I believed in the necessity and inevitability of compromise**. Now I know that compromise causes the lessening of spirit and vibrancy in partners and, eventually, in the marriage. There are other ways to work with differences that strengthen and enliven.

> **I believed that two people were required to transform a relationship.** Now I know it takes only one.

> **I believed in right and wrong.** Often my relationships with others hinged on the right-wrong seesaw. Now I know that to practice being right enough for long enough causes our natural spark for living, and our vital energy and creativity, to decrease. Our mood lowers when we sell our soul to be right. An easier route begins with "What if nobody's wrong? How can we grab hands and create something soul satisfying together?"

I believed my happiness depended on altering my environment. I expected my partner to adjust what he said or did as a first step, rather than modifying my actions or words. Now I know that happiness is mine to create, which means the initial step comes from yours truly, every time. This deepened my satisfaction in being with Eric. To this day, being the initial step continues to support me.

I believed that I was behaving in kind ways. However, some of my behavior turned out to be, at its core, unkind to myself and others. To maintain familiar habits, I blinded myself to the downside of certain ways of relating. Now I know that to live in profound intimacy requires a deep, long, honest-to-the-core investigation about kindness.

When We Take a Closer Look at How We Relate

Making the commitment to improve our connection with another person is actually a pledge to study ourselves. This is a promise that guarantees upheaval. When we begin to examine how and why we withhold information or sidestep the truth, for instance, we discover our fears, which is uncomfortable. When we truly comprehend the impact of criticism, we ache about things we've said or done. If we change our ways, and begin to act with kindness toward friends and family we had sworn ourselves against, we face the realization that we've been as hard on ourselves as we are on others. Instead of holding a negative attitude, we begin to be more curious about and maybe even more responsible for the part we play in relationships with our least favorite relatives and exes. This awakening requires courage and an ongoing commitment. It is not a breeze.

And what about the messy and controversial territories of politics, religion, and philosophy? The pledge to study ourselves means that deliberate and conscious consideration of the attitudes we find offensive becomes our inner work. To surrender our personal superiority changes our brain. It obliges us to accept as respected equals the folks at our family dinner table—the drunken uncle, the ne'er-do-well cousin, the cantankerous grandparent—as well as the people from other cultures or mindsets we don't understand. Each time we're tempted to wag a finger at someone else, we remember to investigate our heart and mind. Rather than explode in anger at another, we first attend to our own healing.

This sounds like serious work, doesn't it? It sounds drastic—perhaps even unattractive, confusing, or impossible. Humbling, for sure. Being willing to inquire within and then make foundational shifts such as these causes disruption and disorientation in ourselves until we find new feet.

At this moment, I'm taking a deep breath right along with you. Transforming any relationship means examining all of these things. This is profoundly personal work. In my own experience, it became clear to me that in the face of difficulty or disagreement, I furnished evaluation, not true curiosity. I didn't look to myself for changes that would make a difference in the quality of my relating. My notions of superiority and inferiority guided me, rather than love and acceptance. My new awareness urged me to examine whether the rules of engagement for Eric and me encouraged lavish participation and joyful expression. Or was one of us dumbed-down or shushed? Was either one of us—ever— persuaded that we were not enough?

My stated desire over the years was to have a good, solid marriage. I would *find one*. I'd meet the right person. However, I didn't know that finding a worthy candidate doesn't guarantee a good marriage. Nor was I aware that learning to love myself was the path to creating an extraordinary love relationship with another. We can only love someone else to the extent that we have compassion and love for ourselves. We don't find a good marriage; we find the skills within us to build one. This book is that path: trust that you have skills, find them, and practice them with enthusiasm.

A Third Something

It turns out that when two people meet and begin to relate, a third something is created that enfolds them both. It's not so much a thing but more of an advantage and a possibility. The profound and fundamental gift that opens itself is the opportunity to become true-you, the you that expresses your Inner Being. True-you is divine (spirit) and human (flesh) as one—your godself.

The gift of relationship allows us to find our stride, to fill the shoes called our most authentic and loving self. Instead of hunting for love, or grasping or hoping for love from others, we get to know the love already within us. We learn the truth of where love comes from, that what we search for is doing the looking. We are the love we seek.

Exercise #1: How You Think About Your Partner

This is a good moment to reflect on how you think about your partner. Make a list of at least twenty items. For each entry, ask yourself whether this way of thinking about your partner makes you content, and put a star next to those that do. Here are some prompts to get you started.

- I'm often upset about...
- My partner makes me laugh when...
- My partner helps me by...
- I hate when...
- I love when...
- At dinner with friends, my partner...
- My partner's health habits...
- My partner's driving habits...
- I admire and respect...
- I shut down when...
- I feel safe when...

After you make a list and add the stars, consider these questions:

1. Do your prevailing thoughts about him/her enliven you?

2. Does your frame of mind about your partner cause you to look forward to time together?
3. Is the way you feel about your partner on most days how you truly want to feel?
4. Are you happy with the time and effort spent on challenges that arise?

Note the existing balance—the number of entries that make you content, relaxed, and happy versus those that don't. If you could use assistance with items on your list, then take my hand and walk with me.

Exercise #2: My Beliefs About Partnership

Next, be committed to the conscious awareness of what you believe about being in a partnership so that you can hold all of it up to the light. For instance, what do you believe about getting along? Put your thoughts on paper.

- My partner should _____. (Ex: My partner should be more interested in other people when we go out to dinner, rather than talking so much about himself.)
- My partner should not _____. (Ex: My partner should not promise something she can't deliver, or doesn't intend to deliver.)
- The quality (or habit) of_____ is important because _____. (Ex: Being on time is important to me because it conveys respect.)
- I need _____ and it looks like _____. My partner's responsibility around that is_____. (Ex: I need to plan ahead for vacations, a total of thirty days off a year. My partner should be willing to help me plan and pay for the vacations, and stick to the plan.)

Keep adding to your list of beliefs as you read. As you find your beliefs, set them aside. No need to give them up. You can have them back any time you like. The beauty of setting beliefs aside temporarily is that it makes simple, clean space to experience a deeper layer of our being. It clears the clutter of what we've told ourselves and what we've accumulated over time. It allows us to wipe the slate and start fresh. As you complete each section of the book, look back at the list to see if any of your beliefs have shifted, loosened, or altered entirely.

Because of your strength, intelligence, and capable nature, I'm addressing the curated, adjusted version of you, dear reader—the version you've expressed until now. Please invite any polished and well-dressed aspects of yourself to sit down and rest, to grant time and space for a deeper and wiser you that stands waiting. By sharing my process, I hope to help you create the transformation you seek. Making personal changes in the direction of love is no small matter. It will require everything you've got.

~~~~~

Let us now try what love will do.
—William Penn

2

Begin—Again

MY WRITING IS for men and women who seek to improve the quality of an intimate connection or partnership. When my words are for women, men learn indirectly. When my words are for men, women learn. Women have an inclination to link arms—we are relationship oriented—and within this familiar relational territory of ours, we also have influence. Because of our innate strength and skill, my work is often directed to women.

To be clear, when my information is directed to women, it makes sense to women, and it helps women. That does not mean my work is aimed at women, as if women are a problem and women need fixing. In fact, what a perfect moment to say that nobody's the problem and nobody needs fixing. Further, what if nobody's wrong? Believing we're wrong backs the best of us into a corner. Disapproval tends to take our breath away. It can cause us to hesitate, to act with unnecessary caution.

A true story about Dr. Hew Len inspired me to practice "what if nobody's wrong." Around 1980, at the Hawaii State Hospital, Dr. Len was assigned to a special ward for the criminally insane. This was a place that housed murderers and rapists, people who had done truly brutal things. Being employed at this facility was intense and dangerous. Patients attacked one another and the staff nearly every day.

Dr. Len was a practitioner of *ho'oponopono*, a Hawaiian approach to the development of community, which involves accepting communal responsibility for individual issues that arise. In ho'oponopono, one person's issue becomes the entire group's. With advice from the group's elders, they find a resolution that is accepted by the whole community. The four steps of this approach involve Repentance (I'm Sorry), Forgiveness (Please Forgive Me), Gratitude (Thank You), and Love (I Love You). The belief is that when individual minds heal, the worldly problem in question heals, too. This may seem like a far-out idea (it did to me at first), but research suggests the results of ho'oponopono are similar to the miracles that occur when a group or an individual holds a person or situation in prayer.

Instead of looking for what was wrong with the patients, Dr. Len pored over one patient file after another. He read the details of their crimes and made peace within himself about what each person had done. It was a slow process. He didn't judge the patients or look for ways to correct them. He did not try to rehabilitate them. In fact, he consciously expressed gratitude for the opportunity they provided to examine himself.

Dr. Hew Len never personally attended to the patients, yet positive changes occurred. Some patients were taken off their medications. Others stopped fighting. Harmony between patients and staff increased. One by one patients were declared well enough to leave the treatment facility, and in fact, at the end of four years, the hospital closed due to lack of business. Only two patients remained, and they were transferred to another facility. This is the story that inspired me to look within as a first step any time I felt upset with Eric.

100 Percent Responsibility

When offering a client consulting session, I speak to a woman as if she is in charge of her partnership. Each aspect is in her capable hands. She gets the respect she deserves (not the blame), which is that *she's it*. She's the one who can turn things around in herself any time she chooses. The world around her will change as a reflection of her inner work. Her conversations, her circumstances, her future possibilities morph as she becomes more true to herself.

When in session with a man, he's presented with the exact same principle. He's in charge of his intimate relationship. He gets the respect he deserves (not the blame), which is that *he's it*. In his work with me, he focuses on being true to himself. He becomes the man he wants to be and knows he is, which helps him personally but also contributes enormously to his intimate relationship.

It's important to understand what responsibility is and is not. Werner Erhard, creator of transformational models and applications for individual, organizational, and social transformation says this:

> Responsibility begins with the willingness to take the stand that one is cause in the matter of one's life. It is a declaration not an assertion, that is, it is a context from which one chooses to live. Responsibility is not burden, fault, praise, blame, credit, shame or guilt. In responsibility, there is no evaluation of good or bad, right or wrong. There is simply what's so, and the stand you choose to take on what's so. Being responsible starts with the willingness to deal with a situation from the view of life that you are the generator of what you do, what you have and what you are. That is not the truth. It is a place to stand. No one can make you responsible, nor can you impose responsibility on another. It is a grace you give yourself—an empowering context that leaves you with a say in the matter of life.[2]

What About Choosing Sides?

In consulting sessions with couples, I don't take sides. I don't believe in sides. Favoring either partner is counterproductive. However, there are matches, as in how does the match between these two people work? What keeps the connection humming along? Relationships are whole—nothing missing, nothing wrong. The woman is the whole relationship, and she has full responsibility. The man is the whole relationship, and he has full responsibility. The person asking the questions and seeking answers has full responsibility, even when a partner is a few inches away listening. You'll be able to follow how this works in the conversations with clients presented in this book.

This fundamental shift made all the difference for me. My old belief was, "Sure, I'll look at my behavior, but let's concentrate on my husband and make sure he fixes things. Then I'll be happy." My sudden epiphany was, "The outcome of my marriage is entirely in my hands." My connection with Eric shifted remarkably, and our love and respect for each other grew. Our life together transformed.

Change Versus Transformation

The difference between change and transformation is relevant to this discussion. Change focuses on modifying actions step by step to achieve a desired result. Transformation, on the other hand, is metamorphic. It is drastic and all-encompassing and causes a caterpillar-to-butterfly effect. We become entirely and suddenly different, so much so that we hardly recognize ourselves.

My marital transformation came about from the cumulative effect of my past failures, along with an added threat on that are-you-done-with-me-yet Sunday morning. It caused a dramatic leap in understanding: "I'm totally responsible for my marriage! All of it." Then my actions changed—they reflected my transformation. Change, though entirely different from transformation, works hand in hand with it. Change supports transformation. I'll speak more about this as we go along.

What Causes Suffering?

Abdicating personal responsibility brought me approximately fifty years of suffering. Why did I suffer? My learned behaviors caused suffering.

Believing my stressful thoughts caused suffering.

It's normal and natural for us to think stressful thoughts. Believing in our stressful thoughts, however, causes suffering. The self-critical thought "I look really bad in this outfit" is humorous if we're light about it. However, if we believe in it, it's stressful. If we notice a negative thought but don't invest in it, then it is simply a thought we're having, rather than a binding truth.

My resistance caused suffering.

If I didn't like what Eric did or said, my habit was to push against him rather than go my own way. This affected me, but also us. My resistance caused suffering in our household, in our bedroom, and in our spirits. Over time we began to say less, participate with one another less, and enjoy each other less. When we didn't confide in one another, or share concerns or questions, this caused suffering in both of us.

I suffered because I took credit when outcomes were triumphant but not when they swerved sideways.

When things tanked, I blamed, often elegantly. Also, I labeled people and situations, as if labeling would somehow relieve me of responsibility and create proof that the problem was someone else's, not mine. My habit was to put failure in others' courts, on their doorsteps, with them rather than with me, and sound reasonably smart and confident while doing it. What I didn't realize was that the use of blame blunted my ability to create my own evolution. This caused years of suffering. After speaking to many well-educated men and women with families, brilliant careers, and years of life experience, what seems true is that the smarter the person, the more reasonable they sound while pointing the finger at a partner, friend, leader, or group.

The Invitation

I am inviting you to uncover the thoughts and habitual behaviors that cause suffering in you. Once apparent, they have less sway. They become one choice among others, rather than reigning as the primary, unconscious default choice. No longer believing in stressful thoughts is a journey where the outcome is not only positive, but it is enlivening beyond anything you may have imagined for yourself. We can do this together.

Have you ever had a serious physical accident? You wonder if your body will ever recover. Will I be able to climb stairs again? Go on hikes? Will this injury haunt me forever? When my knee was seriously injured, my massage therapist reassured me that my knee was fine—but that it was "going through something." It took a while, but my knee did improve. This same idea applies to relationships. No matter how many times we've been married or how trying a relationship has been, our essential soul is fine—it's our personality that goes through something.

Alterations in the way we behave in intimate relationships can be a tall order. Speaking for myself, to take on a complete remodel and transformation in my midfifties was certainly a tall order for me. My journey began with cleaning my mind. As I sorted and swept, there were encounters with my favorite forms of criticism, such as disapproval, judgment, or wishing that Eric was different than he was. When it became clear to me how often I resorted to this, I stopped as best I could. It wasn't enjoyable to feel that way, nor did I relish how my oppositional stance affected him.

There were, of course, small incidents that prompted frustration between us, such as his not doing what he had promised. He'd postponed an errand without letting me know, or he'd forgotten to get back to me about the status of something. But the two of us also had real differences. Living together was as challenging for us as with any couple. Our relationship required work. Things didn't suddenly turn around due to a couple of easy shifts in my thinking, just in case you were wondering.

For Instance

One habit of Eric's was troublesome to me because of its intensity and frequency. His pattern of last-minute trips to the post office to mail pro audio gear for his repair business meant he had to rush. Imagine the ripping sounds of the packing tape dispenser as he hurriedly closed boxes for shipping, along with audible frustration about a misprinted packing label or a lost address. Finally there were hasty footsteps carrying boxes to the van and a high-speed downhill chase to arrive at the post office before it closed. For an hour or two each day, the energy in our home felt frantic. It was impossible for me to concentrate on creative projects during these times, but I didn't speak up. My growing resentment about this daily occurrence spilled sideways into other communications.

Besides the fleeting irritations, Eric and I had larger issues, too. We didn't agree on how to handle money. He refused to plan ahead, especially to allocate or save money, which made me feel as if we were standing on a shabbily built rope-and-board walkway strung across a gaping canyon. Even when we managed to agree on a financial plan, it often didn't pan out. He preferred crisis; I preferred calm. He was prone to urgent, chaotic, adrenaline-filled decisions, and I sought the serenity derived from looking ahead to accommodate life's inevitable surprises.

With these examples in hand, let's circle back to the idea of cleaning the mind and how one commits to "heal thyself" even when a problem appears to be caused by another person. To develop my skills in this effort, I often cleaned and sorted aloud, bold as can be, face-to-face with Eric. He became a witness to certain practices I'd been holding close and using against us.

There were times when I said, "Hey, Eric, I'd like to confess the line of reasoning going on inside my head right now..." Or sometimes we'd point at a crumpled old thing unearthed from my inner closet and we'd talk about it. We'd hang it up on a hanger. Lifting it up into the light of day meant that it was no longer my hidden, raggedy, unkempt, dark-corner thing—it was ours. When things became ours, that made a difference. Together we could toss out my old ways, which affected his old ways, and then they became nobody's ways. We created fresh starts. It was liberating.

No Going Back

Eric was my partner in awareness, and he was good at it—as long as he was rested, fed, and in decent spirits. But if he was tired, grumpy, or hadn't eaten, he'd say, "Can't do that right now. But you can tell me later." He was pretty good at knowing whether he had the bandwidth to hear me.

If critical thoughts strolled into my head when I was alone, I voiced them to an empty room so that nothing slipped by. "Oh, look what I'm doing. I'm yelling at a person in my head." There is a brilliant thing you'll discover if you do this with me. Once you speak your scorn or belittlement, there's no going back. You can no longer pretend not to notice when your attitude is unkind. You can't ignore how it feels to drum up and believe in a bad story about someone. It's impossible to overlook time spent on detrimental or defeatist inner talk, or the effects of it. If you commit yourself to this, the day comes when actions that diminish you or another no longer slip by unnoticed.

Hang It Up

When you're certain that life dealt you a blow, hang up your beliefs about the situation on the clothesline, then step back and take a look. If you're sure your partner has been thoughtless, or doesn't care about you, hang it up on the line. What else could it be? Come up with some possibilities. If your mate blurts a remark that throws you sideways, again, hang it up. Don't assume you're right about what your partner meant—ask! If an open mind leads to an open heart, this is a way to grow one.

My interpretations of Eric's actions, intentions, or words were often incorrect when I based them on my own context. He wasn't me. Eric was raised in Upstate New York. My life began on a farm in Iowa. Eric had a talent for math, electronics, and electricity. My interests center around the sound and feel of nature, the beauty of words, and the importance of feeling joyful and being in the flow. The idea of making a difference in the world motivated Eric. What is valuable to me is harmony, beauty, and creative expression. Eric had stronger muscles than me. He had a different education, different hormones, different hopes and fears—he was distinct from me in every way! My interpretation of him was problematic when it was based primarily on my understanding of myself.

I began to ask more questions. When Eric seemed abrupt toward me, I checked to see whether he was upset about something I'd said or done. When he zeroed in on a project, he didn't talk much. If he did speak, he used few words. What appeared to me as being curt was usually Eric in get-'er-done mode.

The difference between what someone means and what we interpret can become a source of awe and entertainment. Exploring this in an honest and open way builds trust and intimacy. Only by checking did I begin to recognize the difference between *he's ignoring me* versus *he's focused*. Or that his not wanting to join me for an afternoon excursion, or even a vacation, had nothing to do with a desire to avoid me. Rather, something else was calling for his attention. What an emancipating revelation! Much of what I initially took personally turned out to be not the least bit personal, and instead became a source of amusement for both of us. We laughed more—and chances are, if you're reading this book, laughter is something you'd welcome, too.

Don't Let the Past Win

Explore how your beliefs about your partner affect the two of you. For instance, if you treat your husband as if he'll always be the way he was last week, or last year, how does this affect your relationship? If you base your current thoughts, decisions, or feelings on the way you think he's always been, does it prevent or delay positive change? Does your view of him hold the two of you back?

My beliefs about Eric were indeed strong enough to influence our dynamics. One day during a kitchen discussion, he said so: "When you approach me as if I'm the same guy I was five years ago, that keeps us stuck. If I change and you can't see it, the past wins. I can't help me or us. If you see my changes, we can evolve. And I know our evolution is important to you."

Eric's communication stopped me in my tracks. An important choice was in my hands: would he always be the person who made *that* error, said *those* words? Further, how did my treatment of him reflect how I treated myself? Was I as hard on myself as I was on him? Could I adopt a more forgiving view of my past as well?

Let It Fall

Our most tightly held beliefs are often invisible at the beginning of a journey. It takes time to identify them. Personal changes happen more slowly than we wish, over time instead of overnight. But there is one compelling reason why you can accomplish substantial shifts, or even a transformation of your mind and heart: the process requires nothing from anyone else. No one else needs to initiate one single thing.

People around you may begin to evolve along with you, yes—but not because you asked this of them. Through your example, they may recognize their desire for change, along with the strength to make adjustments at their own pace. You being true-you is a standing invitation for others to be true-them.

Keep in mind these three things, and your personal changes will go more smoothly.

> **Relax often.** Trying hard means we believe we're after something that isn't already ours. Pay attention to what's going on—of course! But let there be less sweating about it.

> **Be simple.** My relationship with Eric struck me as complicated at the peak of our difficulties. When things fell apart between us, our situation simplified, which was helpful. Without hesitation, let what falls fall. Simple is good. Sometimes less is better.

> **Travel light.** Using the wood stick insect analogy mentioned in chapter 1, as you climb the redwood, loads of old beliefs fall to the forest floor to become compost. Less baggage leaves more of true-you to do the legwork. Your efforts will feel authentic and satisfying.

There is nothing more inspiring than witnessing two people grow closer, stronger, and happier as time passes. Not only do they get along after years of being together, but they look forward to simple time to walk the dog, play a board game, or take care of a garden. After twenty or thirty years of being grand mixmasters of children, careers, personal challenges, finances, and health, they are best friends with plenty to discuss. Do you know couples like this? I hope you know a few. Even better, become one—still holding hands, still wild about each other after many, many years.

~~~~~

A happy marriage is a long conversation
which always seems too short.
—Andre Maurois

3

Bring Your True-Self

WE WONDER WHY relationships fail. One reason is that entering a relationship as the person you were taught to be (which isn't true-you) attracts a partner who matches not-you (counterfeit you, adjusted you, or curated you). Is it any wonder that a match based on who you learned to be won't make you happy in the long run? The good news is that partnerships provide a stream of opportunities to sort who we think we are from who we actually are. If you're all-in, if you're willing, intimate connections can help you shake off who you learned to be so that you can meet your natural self.

Let's go bone simple. Two clients of mine argued about the trash. She felt strongly that he should take out the garbage and he agreed to do it. However, sometimes he followed through and sometimes he didn't. When irked by his inconsistency, she yelled at him. He resented her and walked away, each time less motivated to help with the trash (or anything else) in the future.

No one is wrong here, by the way. Nobody needs fixing. This couple could do a trash dance for another twenty years. But my question to them was, "Do you enjoy this?" If they could drop the dance in favor of cooperation and satisfaction, would they change it? And where would they start?

The woman realized that one of her routines was to ask (or wish) for something but not receive it. She learned the pattern by being a witness to how it repeatedly played out between her parents, especially during her impressionable years (ages one through seven). She absorbed their pattern thoroughly: through her eyes, her ears, and her gut. In high school, the can't-get-what-you-want template appeared in many forms, one being that she wanted to date but was forbidden. In college, she worked hard but didn't receive the grades she'd hoped for. We made a list of all the ways the pattern turned up. Unfulfilled wishes were everywhere, and of course, this same blueprint played out in her marriage.

In our session, one moment changed her: she realized she was in charge of the existence of the pattern. She was in charge of her perspective. Her change was not step by step—she opened and the truth flew in. It had been waiting for her invitation. It had been waiting for her to throw open the windows and doors—to let the blazing light of the truth of her being come *in*, and come *home*.

Suddenly, she cared less about who did the garbage. Sometimes she removed the garbage herself, but more often than not, her husband did it. When her perspective unlocked, the pressure disappeared, and the garbage issue vanished as if it had never existed. Years of struggle were gone in a matter of hours, because she dropped who she learned to be in favor of the truth of her—true-her!

The Search for True-You

Writer Paulo Coelho said, "Maybe the journey isn't so much about becoming anything. Maybe it's about unbecoming anything that isn't really you, so you can be who you were meant to be in the first place." Finding and being our true selves is the intricate process of first recognizing and then unlearning patterns that don't serve us. It means unlearning who we've become that doesn't work. Becoming true-us means dropping who we were forced to be, who we felt obligated or pressured to be.

For a profound lesson in all of this, read Tara Westover's memoir *Educated*. She was raised by survivalist parents in a Mormon community in Idaho. It's the story of her gradual realization of the difference between who she learned to be versus her authentic self. It's an against-all-odds account of how her upbringing at first thwarted her self-expression and then propelled it.

Concealment is one survival strategy. Perhaps it was one of yours in your youth. You sidestepped fury and flying fists by disappearing where no one could find you, and it literally saved you. You avoided bodily harm by not disclosing your whereabouts. That's a pretty good reason to do what you did.

In your teen years, maybe this concealment strategy helped you avoid things you didn't want to do. You pretended to study by leaving home with a book under your arm but went for a nature walk or to a movie instead. You didn't offer the truth about your activities because the truth—I need fresh air or downtime; my creative muse is calling me—wasn't accepted. Because you were talked out of what you needed, you learned to lie. The use of deception gave you some peace. But as Buddha said, "Three things cannot be long hidden: the sun, the moon, and the truth."

Now you're an adult and married. Though your situation has changed, you've brought along your backpack of trusted survival strategies, and quite regularly you reach into that pack. In your intimate relationship, sharing whereabouts is not something you do. To your mate you seem secretive, but not divulging location details is how you roll. This habit has begun to work against you, though. It's causing problems. You have connection, intimacy, and trust issues with your partner. Of course you do.

Unraveling an avoidance strategy in favor of transparency requires awareness, willingness, and discipline. Begin with the commitment to spot when you're not-you. Pay attention to how and when you conceal. When your mate asks for information, note that it would be useful (or loving, or generous) to provide it. There's no danger here, nothing life-threatening. Nor will the information you offer impede your freedom. Each time not-you weighs in, say (aloud if possible), "There you are!" Once you've given recognition to an old strategy, you're freer to make a deliberate, fresh choice.

Offering details to your mate directs not-you to a back seat. This sounds basic. But to do it requires that you notice not-you, unlearn not-you, and begin to find and express true-you—which is a lot. It's more than it might seem at first glance.

Here's a simple example of noticing not-you. When your partner is late, and you're irritated, pause. Take a breath. Then, before delivering a finger-on-the-trigger retort, check to see if this is a reaction you learned and then repeated many times. Does the irritation belong to true-you or not-you? Take your time. Take a long look. You might be surprised at what you find.

The Willingness to Risk Change—What Will That Buy?

In any inquiry, there are questions about direction and risk. If I evolve, where am I going exactly? What will my efforts buy me? Will I like where this takes me? These questions, of course, can never be answered in advance.

The Golden Buddha statue—nine feet tall, five and a half tons—was at one point covered with a thick layer of clay or stucco (accounts vary) inlaid with bits of glass to prevent it from being stolen by Burmese invaders in the mid-1700s. The plan worked. When the Siamese kingdom of Ayutthaya was destroyed, the figure was ignored and left in the rubble. Over the years, the statue was moved several times, finally to Bangkok. Then, in 1955, it was transported to a new building constructed specifically to house it. During the last part of the move, ropes broke and the statue crashed to the ground, breaking the outer covering. Workers discovered that the Buddha was made of pure gold—nine pieces that fit together with a key.

The story of the Golden Buddha reminds us that true-you may be concealed, but it's there, inside. Happiness is there. Love, satisfaction, and joy are there, and they are bright and beautiful and valuable. The Golden Buddha symbolizes our intact, unchanging essence—our true-self. Each of us finds our authentic self when what's shrouding it falls away. We find it when protection of it shatters. Certain habits of mine (evaluation, judgment) obscured my love for myself and my love for Eric. Only parts of me (and only parts of Eric) met with my acceptance, which is not really love at all. Even though I thought of myself as a loving person, my search for true-me had uncovered irrefutable proof of unloving actions. Once I comprehended this, there was no going back. My defensive covering had crumbled. I was stuck with a shinier, brighter, more aware me.

Standing in Love—What It Does to Your Brain

To unearth my loving self, and to keep that self front and center, it needed a name. I called it *love-anyway*. My commitment stemmed from recognition that I could actually feel love leave me. Sometimes love lifted up out of me or floated out the sides of me. Other times it drained through the bottoms of my feet. Love leaving me was not what I wanted, so I resolved to pay exquisite attention to its presence.

At first, taking steps to find "me that loves" seemed strange. It required strength and devotion to recognize the fear, anger, or disappointment I felt when Eric made a financial decision that caused a negative impact on my future. It required even more strength not to succumb to a reaction, but to ask for love's hand instead. It felt odd to remain loving during a disagreement, when he was rude. Standing in love and consciously asking love to stay with me in situations when I might typically resort to frustration while talking politics felt odd. To remember love-anyway in the middle of judgment was a new sensation. It rearranged my brain.

To stand in love even when someone berates you is a worthy endeavor, but it doesn't mean you need to keep close proximity with that person. If your lover is abusive, to practice love-anyway doesn't mean you let the abuse continue. It means you burn the steady flame of love inside while you get help. Use the fire of love as fuel to get you out of there. This is crucial: you can love-anyway and part ways physically.

Love-anyway means to welcome love's assistance. However, it doesn't mean we gloss over, ignore fact, or become a doormat. This is not an instruction to sweep all that's awful into a pretty pile and pretend it's rainbows and sunshine. Keep your discernment! Trust yourself! Love-anyway doesn't ask us to forgo initiation of changes for our personal benefit. In fact, it summons quite the opposite. To live from a loving place engages self-respect. You'll bow out of things that don't suit you or stand up for yourself in situations where you didn't previously.

You might walk away from overgiving. Your interest in a perpetually negative situation could fade suddenly.

Being not-you never helped you love another, or yourself, not even once. Just like the Golden Buddha, all the pieces of true-you fit together with a key—which is love.

~~~~~

Trust yourself; you know more than you think you do.
—Benjamin Spock

4

Love's Invitation

HAPPILY-EVER-AFTER INCLUDES WAY more than anyone lets on. Many of us could tell a story called *The Shocking Awful Truth About Marriage*. We might reveal how profound disappointments ate away at love, or how a turn of events blindsided us or changed our course. Or perhaps there was denial, a turning away as if hardships didn't exist. Each story, however, would describe the actual everyday—not to mention day after day—experience of being with another human over time. The over time aspect is not that easy. It's not a walk in the park.

Most relationships go through something radical sooner or later. A challenge stops by. Bad news drops in. Something sizable shows up because expansion is the essential nature of partnership with another person. To communicate, keep house, make love, have babies, create livelihoods—all of these invite what's in us to rise up singing, and it's not always a happy tune. Relating to another person petitions the hidden, the unknown, and the unexpected to come crawling out of the hidden corners of our most sacred closets. Partnerships issue a continual stream of invitations to evolve. They deliver hard work, guaranteed!

Being in love could be compared to participation in the Relationship Olympic Games. Opening ceremonies are celebrated, and the torch is lit. At a full run, into the two-person Love Bobsled we leap. Strapped in tight, here comes the first curve of the track. Whether we're navigating a slippery downslope on skinny blades or steering our way through a sensitive communication with our lover, we see pretty quickly how we fared.

What most couples don't know, not really, not in their bones, is that challenges help us become *us*. Here's a poem that speaks to this from my book *100 Words: Small Servings of Whimsy and Wisdom to Calm the Mind and Nourish the Heart*.

THE SCOOP ON TRUE PARTNERSHIP
by Terri Crosby

Why bother to save a marriage on the rocks?

Perhaps it would be smarter to start over.
Get something shiny and new, like with shoes or a car.

Why be in a relationship? Do you know why anyone
gets together with another to create a joined life?

One answer rules: We think it will make us happy.
But often it doesn't.

What if marriage is about rising up to become
your best *you*? If true, this intent is not accomplished in

idyllic circumstances. One must be questioned, opposed,
challenged.
Now isn't that partner of yours helping more than you
thought?

~~~~~

Small Is Mighty

Given that relationships have challenges, how can we best work with them? The idea of leaping over tall problems in a single bound has appeal. But when it comes to an intimate relationship, think putt-putt golf. Get a putter and practice short shots.

For many of us, small steps sound tedious. Leapfrogging a Grand Canyon–size problem inch by inch, day after day can seem a paltry, sad effort. But along with everything else to rethink as you move through these pages, maybe this is a good time to reassess the merit of minor steps. Beginning in the slightest way, observe how tiny steps work for other people. We've seen friends make significant progress over months and years by doing a little at a time. They earned university degrees, lost weight over the winter, learned the Argentine tango, or planned trips to faraway destinations. Leaders we admire, such as Lynne Twist (*The Soul of Money*) or Father Gregory Boyle (*Tattoos on the Heart*), clearly value incremental progress. To raise abundance consciousness, as Lynne has done, or to address community violence by opening a bakery staffed by gang members, as Father Boyle has done, requires the appreciation of slow and steady advances. And so begins our tentative relationship with miniature steps.

Being a new student of "small is mighty" means that occasionally we jump too far, back up, and try again. We remind ourselves that tiny steps are s-m-a-l-l and that s-m-a-l-l is good. One initial petite step could be to attend to thoughts. To simply be aware—no action and no adjustment. In quiet moments, where do your thoughts go? While walking the dog, what happens in your head? How does your mind spend free time as you brush your teeth or get undressed for bed? For a week or two, pay extra attention. The next small step could be to observe whether a thought is stressful, simply yes or no. If a thought is stressful, practice doing or saying something that helps you feel a little better right then and there. You can drink water, hum a silly tune, stretch or shake your body, or walk outdoors for a break. Deliberate, small actions help you feel better in the moment. They offer ease. Ease makes good things possible.

My appreciation of micro steps grew over time because the use of them helped me feel happier. They helped me feel like the me I wanted to be. They reinforced new behaviors bit by bit, thought by thought, feeling by feeling, and made me feel more surefooted with myself and with Eric. A profound understanding blossomed from my small-step practice: it became clear to me that what Eric said or did was never the true cause of my stress. What I thought about what he said—my interpretation of his words—is what mattered.

How Can This Work for You?

Let's say you're frustrated about not having enough time to talk to your partner. The two of you speak in sound bites more than sentences. What steps could help with this? A thought to yourself such as "I'd like to make this work" could give reassurance or offer a momentary sense of calm. "I trust that I can figure this out as I go" might be true for you and give you some breathing space. "I look forward to more time together" could work. These are simple steps in the direction of ease. Choose statements that are credible for you.

If you're upset about something your partner has done, how might you small-step your way to relief? The last thing you probably feel able to do is to think all positive and pretty. Please don't be tempted to paste dabs of fake contentment on top of deep disappointment. Don't cover up sad or furious with fake-lovely and expect it to make a valuable difference. Instead, relax your body and your breath. From that place, do your best to begin to receive what the other person did or said.

If you experienced a conversation as harsh, lean toward ease by telling the story to yourself using facts only, until you can cite it without blame or animosity. For example, instead of "He yelled at me and made me feel terrible" you'd say, "His voice had volume as he said [these words]." This will begin to soften the edges of what you heard and felt. State facts until your reaction subsides. Then you can take a short stride toward accepting their actions and words. You can walk toward why the person deserves love-anyway. This method will be covered in more detail in part three.

Here are examples of tiny steps to which clients committed and which made a difference to them over time:

- Stop telling disempowering stories to girlfriends about my relationship—that nothing will ever change or that my hands are tied because of my partner.

- Make time to enjoy pleasant, sensual activities with my partner more often. Schedule date night, go dancing, eat delicious food together.
- Stop jumping to conclusions. Take a breath, then ask questions. Slow down.
- Praise where I can praise. Express gratitude to my children for simple things.
- Catch myself when I compare this husband to my last.
- Don't retaliate when my mate says something inflammatory. Don't pick up the negative stick and throw it back.

Your first go at getting through a conversation about finances, the children's education, or next year's vacation might not work. It's okay. The key is don't stop. Keep relating, and keep taking micro steps. Today's flop is invaluable feedback. Failures contribute to success. Ask any inventor.

Small steps added together over months and years matter. They affect our long-term well-being, whether it's an exercise routine we maintain easily or an awareness practice to catch and shift the habit of a cynical response to the latest political disaster or to the trials of online dating. Putting new habits into practice little by little creates adjustments in how you feel and who you become.

What a pleasure to express true-you a little more each day!

~~~~~

The man who moves a mountain begins
by carrying away small stones.
—Confucius

5

You're a Match

EVERY RELATIONSHIP IS a holy laboratory. The people we marry are our ideal lab partners. There are compelling reasons why two individuals are pulled together: partners match. However, if we're having difficulty with our partner, there's the rub! How could we be in perfect lockstep with the person we want to divorce? How is it possible to be a match to the husband we oppose? How can we be perfectly linked to the person we speak against daily, to the partner we've declared (multiple times to multiple people) we should leave?

A *match* is a person (or thing) able to contend with another as an equal in quality or strength. A match in a partnership creates a cycle of relating, a balanced loop, whether the relating is pleasant or difficult.

Here are two versions of a match:

1. **Pleasant Relating:** One partner loves the other in a free and delightful way. The receiving partner opens to the love and returns it. The first partner welcomes that and offers even more. Their intimacy grows. They match!

2. **Difficult Relating:** One partner requests a conversation. The second partner ignores. The first partner insists more vehemently, and in response, the second ups their pushback. The partners fit together, although not happily. Without changes from either

person, the heat continues and may even intensify. They hold each other in an unpleasant loop. They match.

Two friends of mine who owned a business together had an approach-avoidance match. When there was disagreement, she requested conversations, but he avoided. She was convinced that their meetings would produce valuable solutions, but her husband saw no such chance. In his opinion, her requests to communicate centered around him being at fault. He was certain that no agreement to convert to her way of thinking would adjust matters long-term. It seemed there would always be more to fix. She became frustrated and angry. He turned sullen, cold, and unwilling. Love waned and sexual intimacy disappeared. It was a cyclical, miserable loop. Neither person was open to changing their tune. They matched perfectly.

My Match with Eric

Knowing that you match your partner is helpful, but knowing exactly how you match is key. In the early crash-and-burn months with Eric, when I glimpsed the perfection of our connection, it was more than a little upsetting. One aspect of our basic match was that when I judged him, he took my words to heart. Each time he absorbed my evaluations, he became less confident. To attempt to recover, he defended himself and blamed back. The more debilitated he became, the more there was to disapprove of, which loaded me with further reasons to be frustrated with him, and the cycle rolled on. We were a match.

For so long my secret inner attitude was that if there was trouble between us, we were not compatible, and not a match. But one day a new thought registered: "Wait a minute. If I'm so great, what's a woman like me doing with a terrible, awful, inadequate guy? If I'm cool and right as rain, then what's Mr. Not-Great doing in my life?" Did I need to denounce him in order to feel better about myself? (Apparently.) Was it true that by dubbing him "less than," I could be "more than"? (You bet.)

How off-the-mark to attempt to reinforce my self-worth by reducing his! What would it be like, I wondered, to no longer compare or evaluate? What if we were simply equals learning from each other?

What if we stood toe-to-toe, each doing our best? Those questions brought chunks of stucco crashing to the floor. It was a shining Buddha moment!

My new plan was to become aware of the feeling of criticism in my body as it came up, and to stop on a dime. Doing so helped me see our circular pattern. Eric expressed the self he learned to be (someone who takes in criticism), which matched the self I learned to be (someone who dishes it out). We played predictable though unsatisfying roles with each other, our pattern glued tight by mutual blame.

During this exploration, it became obvious that my use of criticism was often my awkward attempt at feeling safe around men in general, and Eric in particular. Criticism (used in the sense that the best defense is offense) helped me feel able to handle someone who could potentially use his strength (financial, physical, mental) against me. But putting Eric in a defensive position didn't disarm him or protect me; it brought out the worst in him. It defeated him and provoked his anger. It disabled him. It caused him to throw in the towel and give up.

Another habit of mine was to label others, implying their inferiority. By giving Eric a label (he's messy, doesn't understand me, is failing), then *he* had a problem—I didn't. Throwing trouble away from me was a Hail Mary, a long shot, in hopes of feeling more confident and in control. When I stopped doing or saying what diminished Eric, it left me standing squarely in my own game.

My miscalculations affected both of us, because (by criticizing and labeling) I had overlooked our humanity—our strengths and frailties, and our willingness to learn from each other if given a chance. I stopped hurting Eric when I learned kindness for myself. I was blown away by who men are and what they provide for those they love. With new eyes and new ears, I was blown away by women, too, by our compassion, our strength, and our fire.

Becoming the person I am rather than the one I had learned to be opened me, and then—Eric! This is the magic of the ripple effect of one person being true-them. In particular, I interrupted the stressful thought that anything was wrong with either one of us. This helped me relax into being equals who learn from each other. The placement of my attention solely on my behavior was a new discipline, and it released the expectation that his changes would be the ones that made my world better.

How About You?

How does the information so far apply to you and the way you move with your partner? How does being a match to your partner sit with you? Or how about the idea of you as the transformer of your relationship?

For some encouragement, here's a story with a happy ending. It's an account of how my client observes herself by noting what's currently true, then gradually takes responsibility for an outcome she prefers. By learning to distinguish between moments when she is and is not herself, she initiates actions that are new for her and in line with her true-self. In time her changes modify the dynamics of the entire family in a positive way. She creates a new match.

> At work she focused on constant improvement. She was hired to anticipate problems and solve them before they grew and was paid well for this skill. As a futurist, she examined historical data with the goal of predicting future trends. She studied "what if" scenarios and recommended appropriate proactive preparation.
>
> However, when she engaged that same talent at home, the focus on constant improvement backfired. Her mate and children felt as if nothing they did was enough. There was always a goal in the air, something that needed to be better than it was. Life together had become about striving and accomplishment and not so much about delight or celebration.
>
> Her children wished for time to play freely, goof around, be spontaneous. They wanted to dream up costumes or go on summer picnics by the river, not tackle yet another mom goal. Her young ones were stressed and had become increasingly serious, guarded, and uncooperative around her.

Her husband felt underappreciated and overlooked. The spark they had felt at the beginning of their relationship dimmed as the daily scramble to keep up with her push for excellence took increasing priority. He preferred time at home to be casual and fun-loving. He adored her and wanted to take simple walks to connect. He felt his affection for her no longer made a difference.

In sessions with me, her first assignment was to observe each family member as if they'd never met—who are they, what do they naturally enjoy? At our next meeting, she reported that when left to their own devices, her youngsters watched the clouds move, explored the woods, or talked to her about what birds did. When they were not hurried along, they sat on their haunches and observed ants on a sidewalk, dabbled in paint, or paused in their pajamas to exclaim about the pattern of moonlight on their bed. They were kids who enjoyed the natural world, which she decided was a good thing. She described her husband as "a little bit lonely."

Through her relaxed investigation, she discovered her willingness to let her family educate her. Over dinner she asked her husband and children to teach her how to have more fun. Their answer? "Yes, we will!"

The result? Her partner's confidence and enthusiasm returned. Her children were excited to have time with their "real mom." That was the name they gave her, and it encouraged her to continue learning. All five of them were delighted to feel connected to one another and enjoy one another more.

The over-the-top bonus? Her children are growing up as true-them. This is the value of tending to our side of any match. We walk toward love, and others join us.

The Simple Wonder of "Thank You"

In order to unravel an old habit, another client made the decision to express more appreciation toward others. She said it was a place that felt jammed in her—backed up, confusing, and awkward. She wanted to discover who she had learned to be and practice less of that. She wondered what it might be like to be true-her.

As a child in her large Kentucky farm family, she worked hard. Expectations were high, but pats on the back and words of praise were rare. She and her brothers and sisters worked in the garden. They fed chickens, gathered eggs, and helped take care of farm animals and crops. Hard work was required, but the thanks for it was, at most, a silent nod. For her, gratitude lived in food prepared or in fire's warmth in winter but not so much in people.

In her budding appreciation practice, she focused on her husband. At first it seemed fake to express gratitude for things she had never thanked him for. Like the Tin Man in *The Wizard of Oz*, she squeaked each time she moved her itty-bitty muscle of appreciation.

"Thank you for picking up groceries."
"Thank you for seeing that I needed help with this."
"Thank you for listening. Expressing myself helped me find my next move."

She joked that to thank him felt so excessive it made her nauseous. For relief, she sometimes took to acting dramatically reluctant, which entertained them both. When she shared reactions, her husband welcomed them. Why did she need to thank him for *that*? Why did he deserve *that*? When her mind insisted, "It's not fair," she often gave him a brief attitude report. He loved her candor. Also, he was her partner in awareness. He was not her policeman or scorekeeper. (This is important. If your partner can't be neutral, find another awareness buddy.)

Because their interactions were confessional, vulnerable, and humorous, the two of them rekindled their intimacy. They held hands as they did when they first met and were more playful with each other. They flirted frequently and made love more often.

She left behind who she was taught to be in favor of true-her. Her past with her family had informed her that silent appreciation was surely good enough, as in "since when do you need to be thanked for something you're expected to do?" It hadn't occurred to her to consider another way of being. Now, however, her relationship with her husband had provided the impetus to evolve past what she had picked up during childhood. Her new endeavor was clear: keep thanking, keep noticing, keep learning. She preferred to open her mind and grow her heart.

She continued to observe herself, no matter what. She didn't abandon her commitment to express appreciation when inner reluctance, pouts, or protests surfaced. To become aware of her habits and attitudes around thankfulness would eventually allow her to alter this pattern she no longer wanted. Thinking the exercise was an unnecessary waste of time came up pretty often, but she reminded herself that it takes one person to transform a relationship. Thanking her husband would help her, and helping her would cause a positive ripple effect for both of them.

By the way, you can learn to appreciate more fully by appreciating yourself, or someone else. The starting block matters not at all, because when appreciation is given, it expands through any available path. As voicing acknowledgment becomes easier, you'll enjoy how it feels to take the lid off your self-expression, and you'll be touched by what your words of gratitude do for those who receive them. You'll open up love in other ways, too, even with total strangers, if you attend to your side of the match.

How Changing the Present Affects the Past

When changing a long-held belief, it's not unusual to wonder whether altering our behavior now implies that we were wrong in the past. But there are wider views of this, one being that current changes affect the past in a magnificently positive way, bringing even more joy to the present.

It's a good time for another story. When strong, savvy, spirited women begin to look back at their childhoods to see who they learned to be, it's common for them to feel that at least one parent was overly cautious and protective. Such women describe being reined in, held back from what they wanted to do or who they wanted to be. One client related that she'd applied to be a summer intern in Congress without her father's knowledge and was accepted, but her father had refused to let her go. After our conversation, she realized that the foundation for his actions might have been different from what she had originally imagined. Rather than him being "hell-bent on controlling her," perhaps he was focused on protection. He felt directly responsible for her safety.

This new possibility modified her interpretation of the past with her father. He was likely doing his best to shield her from situations where her innocence may have been at stake. By the end of our session, she knew the truth in her bones. He loved her, cared about her, and had carried out his commitment to keep her safe in the best way he could. With this discovery, her resentment of him fell away. An unexpected change took place at work, too. She found male coworkers and bosses to be more receptive toward her and described them as "more relaxed, more conversational." Opinions about men no longer in sync with her true-self began to drop away on their own. She had created a new match.

One final reflection involves yours truly. Before working in this focused way with myself, I would have been squeamish about the disclosure of personal stories shared with you so far. I would have omitted questionable behaviors of mine or glossed over the admission that I thought of myself as a kind person, even though some of my actions turned out to be unkind at the core. It would have been easy to disguise an unflattering situation by attributing it to someone else in order to maintain a comfortable view of myself, and hope that you saw me in a favorable light.

However, in those turn-myself-around years, it became especially clear that I'm not fond of pretending to be someone other than who I am. My preference is to live transparently—to reveal mistakes made as well as the benefit gleaned from them. Brené Brown's advice seems true, that "owning our story and loving ourselves through that process is the bravest thing we'll ever do." Rather than gloss over the fact that I'm a relationship coach who's been married four times, it's productive to share it so the experience can help you as well. It's my belief that we don't inspire others by being perfect. We inspire others by being real.

Talking truth strengthens us and lets us sleep well. When you are forthright and lean into true-you, your life will change in positive ways you might not be able to imagine. Here's to your dance toward true-you!

~~~~~

Be yourself, everyone else is taken.
—Oscar Wilde

Even
when
we know
what
works,
there's
the rather giant matter
of actually doing it.

6

Choose to Do What Works

PERSONAL CHANGES OFTEN begin with a disruptive prompt, a quake of sorts, which births an epiphany. There's a sudden, seismic shift in understanding. Things open up, and ready or not, energy from the quake shoves us forward into a new version of ourselves.

Andi had been struggling with her boyfriend. She received a poem from a friend, called "For Love in a Time of Conflict" by John O'Donohue[3], which begins, "When the gentleness between you hardens..." When Andi read these words, something happened. The poem went straight to her grasp of things and untied all the perfect bows.

By the time she'd read to the end, beliefs of hers had loosened. Some had fallen away. She felt undone, freer to think and be. That same day, she met with her boyfriend and let her hair down. Agreement with him was now less important than cooperation around their differences. Something as simple as a poem shook her, changed her. There was no way back to where she once was. She had moved too far. She had transformed.

Transformation is not an end, however. It's a beginning. After transformation comes work, the part where we fall down, get back up, and try again. Jewish mystic and healer Baal Shem Tov said, "Let me fall if I must. The one I will become will catch me." Andi's post-quake work was intense for her. It's a good thing we have as many tries as we need. No one is counting.

Slow Change Versus The Big Whoosh

Whether you improve a connection with your partner through deliberate change-steps, or a transformation heaves you headlong into a realization that upends you, both methods contribute mightily to realizing true-you.

Change is slower: intentional, eyes wide-open, small steps. Transformation happens radically, seemingly outside time and space. Change sometimes leads to transformation. Transformation certainly leads to change. Change and transformation have one thing in common: both need support.

Transformation often occurs around tragic experiences—profound failure, sudden loss, or the threat of loss. These are powerful transformation setups. We transform because of the death of a partner, for instance, or due to a near-death experience of our own. In my second marriage, my husband announced he wanted a divorce because the *me* I had offered didn't work for him. He said that I had not turned out to be the woman he expected or wanted. He was hoping for a partner who would sit lovingly in the background, focused on supporting him in business. By being asked to do this, I also realized that I was not the wife he was hoping for.

His departure sent me to my knees for nine months—or was it years? And though to describe it as a struggle is an understatement, important truths were revealed. At the time, his actions felt critical and hurtful, but the great advantage in retrospect is that he did me a favor by calling a halt to our marriage. If a relationship doesn't work for one partner, it doesn't work for either partner. I would never be the person he needed and wanted, and by bowing out, he released us from further failure and suffering. He forced me to own up to true-me.

When he moved out, the floor of my existence vanished without warning, and the experience shocked me, transformed me, opened me. A radical transformation requires substantial support. To continue my daily schedule of relationship work, I needed to find ways to cushion the blow of his exit. Welcoming the company of good friends and getting more sleep went to the top of my self-care to-do list.

Navigating Change

Even when we know exactly what to change, still we must decide to take a new step and do it for the first time. To get the result we've declared, we must continue with steps.

To forge a fresh path instead of reacting to our partner in a contrary way requires that we make a deliberate choice to pause and breathe deeply instead. And get curious—ask questions rather than accuse. Reach out rather than retreat. Wake up instead of go numb. Accept what is before us rather than pine for something else. To make a change requires that we be awake and deliberate, over and over.

It's easy to become discouraged if we're unaware that making even a small change changes every part of us. Dr. Joe Dispenza, international lecturer, researcher, and modern-day mystic, puts it this way: "If you want a new outcome, you will have to break the habit of being yourself and reinvent a new self."[4]

To shift, we must actually become the person who can perform a new action (let the desire to retaliate pass), express a new quality (be kind under stress), develop a skill (listen rather than plan a rebuttal), or feel relaxed and confident (around our partner's loud, unruly family). We must become the person who thinks and feels in a way that matches what we're asking for. Yes, take pause here. Change is no small matter. It has layers, and it takes time.

Who we are in this moment is deeply rooted—even more than we might comprehend. Body processes that help us memorize are a handy feature while learning to play the bassoon, but these same systems make it a challenge to alter a habit, a thought pattern, or a way of being. Here are examples of shifts we may not have made, ones where we know better but haven't yet done better.

1. Sighing loudly after a difficult discussion will not help matters with my lover, and still, I sigh.
2. Criticizing my partner when she's already down for the count only makes things worse, and yet I do it anyway.
3. Becoming upset that my husband didn't do something he guaranteed he would do doesn't contribute, and still, I have a meltdown.

4. Complaining to my friend about my mate never produces a happy result, yet I fall back on the habit of telling a "woe-is-me" tale, especially after a couple of glasses of wine.

5. Turning my back to my wife and going straight to sleep because she's done something I disagree with doesn't work, and yet I do it.

Why do what I've always done? Why be loyal to a habit that's not ultimately to my benefit?

Am I weak willed?

No.

Is it that I can't change?

No.

Well, is it that I'm a hopeless case?

Heck no.

What's wrong with me?

Nothing. You're working perfectly. You're the *you* you've been rehearsing. You've practiced being, doing, and thinking your way for years. Body-mind patterns are memorized and automatic.

From Dr. Joe Dispenza:

Psychologists tell us that by the time we're in our mid-30s, our identity or personality will be completely formed. This means that for those of us over 35, we have memorized a select set of behaviors, attitudes, beliefs, emotional reactions, habits, skills, associative memories, conditioned responses, and perceptions that are now subconsciously programmed within us.[5]

How We Learn

Remember the first time you got behind the wheel of a car? You opened the door and slipped into the seat. Then came a deep breath about guiding a hunk of metal between the lines. As you placed the key into the ignition—wait, what comes first? My hands, my feet? You can probably recall the awkwardness of body parts tackling an unfamiliar action set. But later that year, as you entered your vehicle, you were swept into a learned sequence. You were on automatic.

A pattern is a pattern because it is a well-rehearsed collection of body processes. In 1949, Donald Hebb, a Canadian psychologist influential in the area of neuropsychology, sought to understand how the function of neurons (transmitter cells that relay information) contribute to psychological processes such as learning. He presented the idea that repeated practice creates a growth process in cells firing together that facilitates the chances of that same pattern happening again. Hebbian theory states that neurons that fire together are wired together.[6]

Each time we learn something new, the body concocts a never-before-created chemical cocktail. The brain thinks a thought, which produces a corresponding set of chemicals. These chemicals are released into the body, and as they circulate, they find their places (called receptors) and latch on. These chemicals instruct the body how to feel, so that how we think and how we feel match.[7] As the pattern is repeated, cells that fire together become wired together, making it easier to remember new steps without so much effort or concentration. When the process smooths out, we feel a completion, a mission accomplished, because our think-feel-do all match.

When it comes to revising a set of actions, the same focused, conscious, consistent effort required to learn the skill is required to alter it. Upgrading a tennis serve means repetition of the new serve until it becomes natural. Upon his return to Earth, astronaut Chris Hadfield relearned how to speak because gravity caused him to once again feel the weight of his lips and tongue![8] To change anything, practice is necessary, and at first the process feels unpolished or cumbersome.

When Small Grows Big

Most everything that turns awful in a relationship starts small. At first, the dismissal of my partner's requests to talk seems incidental. But if I do it often, it becomes a remembered sequence. Ignoring him gathers predictability and impact. Today he tells me about his evening at basketball with his buddies, and I pretend to hear him while I declutter the living room. He's pretty sure I'm otherwise engaged but shares his story anyway, because he adores me and wants to connect.

But I turn away. My justification for inattention is that there are too many undone tasks. He wants to stand around and talk. *Can't he see I need help here? Is he an idiot? Is it that he doesn't care enough to notice? Maybe he doesn't love me. He's so self-centered.*

A dual punishment follows. My resentment affects both of us, because whatever I do to admonish him also hurts me. It's impossible to think badly about him without inflicting stress on myself. This is how withholding attention can start small with my partner, lock in, and grow until it derails our relationship.

There is much to learn here. First, we often overlook the cost of anger or frustration. James M. Barrie, Scottish novelist and creator of Peter Pan says, "Temper is a weapon that we hold by the blade." When I aim resentment at my partner, both of us pay. Further, in a pattern of inattention, nobody wins. Though tendrils of disappointment and dissatisfaction grow slowly, they also grow steadily. Instead, turn it around. Here are three ways:

1. Touch your partner. Get attention physically. Then talk.
2. Establish eye contact. Then talk.
3. Ask for attention when your partner clearly has it to give. If there aren't enough minutes to discuss an issue, set a future time. That's not only the kind thing to do, but it works for both of you. Words from him, "Can I tell you this story, and then I'll help clean up the living room?" would also be a brilliant solution. Or from her, "I'd love to hear your story, but I'm über-distracted. Can you tell me at dinner when I'll be able to enjoy you more?"

When everybody's paying attention, everybody wins.

Why Practice the Positive?

Engaging in enjoyable activities invigorates our spirit and makes it more likely that we're able to receive what the next twenty-four hours of living will bring. Having extra pleasure in our day fills our emotional, mental, and physical banks with "happy," a resource we draw on when challenges arise. Banked pleasure helps us stay out of the quicksand.

1. **Do what nourishes and sustains you.** Appreciate Earth's beauty. Go for walks in nature. Bow out of things when you need to. Have faith that things will work out. Play with a Hula-Hoop. Get some sun. Watch movies that make you laugh.

2. **Amplify the positive.** Celebrate progress you've made— anywhere, anytime. Focus on what's working or what would work. Share with a friend the value of the novel you're reading, the garden you planted, or an inspiring favor a caregiver did for your mother.

3. **Invite your senses out to play.** Let your eyes linger on a colorful blanket of wildflowers on the side of a mountain. Walk through the morning fog and feel moisture on your eyelids. Put your feet mindfully on cool evening grass. Feel the temperature of the clay in your hands. Practice Tai Chi by the ocean. Stretch as many muscles as possible while walking from one room to another. Enjoy the leaves fluttering in the setting sun as you savor a plate of food. Swim naked under the stars. After lunch on your patio, lie on the ground and watch the clouds. Feel the air moving across your skin, how even the smallest hairs on your arm can sense it.

One Way To Speed Things Up

Let's say you wish to take better care of yourself physically, in particular to pay attention to how your voice indicates your emotional state. You'd like your partner to give you a signal when you exhibit a harsh tone (if you don't catch it first), because a harsh tone means you're hurting or stressed, and you'd like to move toward ease instead.

Come up with an agreed-upon code word or words (for your partner to use) that will provide the feedback you desire. Do this so you don't feel criticized or corrected. Use a term that stands out. It's even better if the words make you laugh. (Clients have used "honey bunny" or "hot tamale" as code words inserted into a silly sentence, for instance.) You can also agree on a simple phrase such as "there it is." Eric usually said code words to me in a light or flirty way, which made his feedback palatable. It's paramount that no judgment is associated with a code word.

At home, Eric said code words aloud, because I requested it. In public, he gave me a signal invisible to others, such as reaching under the table at dinner to squeeze my leg. Or, if we were standing, he'd place his hand on my lower back and gently press a finger to my skin. And yes, sometimes his feedback annoyed me. It's not fun to be caught in the act of repeating an old behavior. However, as soon as possible, I thanked him. After all, he gave me feedback I'd specifically asked for, and because of him, I learned faster. Eric never gloated about feedback. He gave neutral reports, not negative votes. He didn't keep score or pretend that he was perfect and I wasn't. He genuinely wanted to help me, and I was genuinely grateful.

Hopefully, the science in this chapter has conveyed the depth and breadth of change, and has given you understanding and hope going forward. Go out there. Help each other. Be kind. Use your newfound grasp of things to benefit you, and the two of you. You have the power to evolve anything you choose.

~~~~~

Change before you have to.
—Jack Welch

7

Everything About You Is Working

LEFT TO YOUR own devices, you make decisions and course-correct. Through experimentation, you determine what brings out the best in you. You assess what makes you shiny-happy and what doesn't.

However, inborn knowledge and the encouragement to act on that knowledge are often cast out of us by protective adults who hope their brand of intelligence and experience will save us from missteps. Which...doesn't work. Because there's *you*—the you who came here to be *you*. No doubt the adults who steered your growth had reasons to curtail you. Without them keeping you in check, you'd have been incorrigible. Full expression *of you from you* would have been inconvenient, time-consuming, and probably uncomfortably revealing about them as parents.

Here's the biggest problem with you being you: if you know who you are, no one can control you. You'd refuse to do what holds no interest. It would be impossible to shame you, inflict obligation, or limit you. You'd choose an occupation and lifestyle to match what inspires you, not necessarily what others hope you choose. Can you imagine what a different world this would be if we managed to retain more of who we naturally are? We'd be less fearful, more confident. Less painfully polite, more forthright. We might speak more kindly about ourselves. We might even believe in ourselves.

Your Inner Being Offers Inner Guidance

Your Inner Being is the higher intelligence lifestream called "you." It is the presence in you that offers guidance toward the expression of true-you. Author and educator Howard Washington Thurman says, "There is something in every one of you that waits and listens for the sound of the genuine in yourself. It is the only true guide you will ever have. And if you cannot hear it, you will all of your life spend your days on the ends of strings somebody else pulls." The life you came here to live comes from being you, trusting you. So yes, by all means, listen to you.

Inner Guidance is offered by your Inner Being through nudges, urges, random thoughts, dreams, emotions, and inspiration. Guidance is available whether or not we pay attention to it. When ignored, it idles. It never abandons us, but it's possible to think that we are apart from it.

Your Inner Being holds the big picture. It will never call you wrong for spouting angry words yesterday or give two thumbs up for the necessity of today's drudgery. Instead, our Inner Beings align with the ease of loving ourselves. Inner Beings nudge us, for instance, to consider a game of Frisbee with our dog and then resume a task with a lighter outlook.

We can dismiss our Inner Being, or form a partnership. We can brush off the signal or take the hand it's offering. Let's say you're at work, and there's an email from your boss asking for the rewrite of a report you labored over. After reading the request, you notice self-judgment, which feels uncomfortable. Drawing a negative conclusion about yourself (or your boss) lowers your mood and increases body tension. This is, shall we say, guidance at work.

Research shows that thinking tends to initiate a loop effect: my thinking creates a feeling, which keeps me thinking the way I'm thinking, and then I'm in a loop. I think the way I feel, and feel the way I think. A happy thought produces a feeling of elation. A disparaging thought creates an unpleasant sensation.

Your Inner Being never agrees with a gloomy opinion about your value as a person, but it will support you by creating emotions that match your thoughts. Self-judgment is a signal that you've thought yourself separate from love. This signal can be seen as a wake-up to change course if you choose. What a perfect guidance system! What a gift!

Keep in mind that guidance from within doesn't mean protection from learning. Struggles and stumbles are a natural part of being a spirit in a physical body. Every human being experiences failed attempts and do-overs. Our assignment is to make room for what shows up, and learn, baby, learn.

What Looks Wrong Could Actually Be All Right

Sir Ken Robinson, British author and speaker, tells a story about a school that wrote to the parents of a little girl, Gillian, to inform them of her possible learning disorder. She couldn't concentrate. She fidgeted, her homework was usually late, and she had a tendency to disturb others in class. The school recommended that the mother take Gillian to a specialist.

Gillian sat on her hands for twenty minutes while Mom and the doctor discussed her school problems. The doctor then turned to Gillian, saying he needed to speak to her mother privately, and asked Gillian to wait in the room. Before walking out, the doctor turned on his desk radio. Once out of the room, they watched her through a window. In no time at all, Gillian was out of her seat dancing. Turning to the mother, the doctor said, "You know Mrs. Lynne, Gillian isn't sick. She's a dancer. Take her to a dance school."

Gillian Lynne did indeed go to dance school. She described how wonderful it was to meet a group of people like herself—people who couldn't sit still, people who had to move in order to think. Gillian went on to the Royal Ballet, met Andrew Lloyd Webber, and became the choreographer for *Cats* and *Phantom of the Opera*. Gillian has brought joy to millions.

It would be truly revolutionary if each child born was given a fair and honest chance to express Inner Guidance. How star-spangled it would be if teachers and parents waved a flag for the idea that nothing's wrong with a young one. Like Gillian, each child born has something special and worthy of support, waiting to be expressed. We could help them find it.

What's So Positive About Being Negative?

It might sound strange to say that negative thoughts have a positive influence, but I have found this to be true. By thinking unkindly about Eric and noticing the accompanying (emotional) signal from my Inner Being, I became ultra-aware of my preference to be kind. After all, who wouldn't prefer kindness if it was an authentic possibility?

Negative thoughts and emotions guided me toward true-me and toward the life with Eric that I wanted, to have more fun with him, laugh out loud, and learn from each other. Painful emotion became a touch on my shoulder to pay attention. It was an intimate and loving reminder to choose to be the person I am.

Negative emotion is good, solid assistance and the best, most reliable coaching we could ever hope for. When irritation at someone else or disappointment in ourselves becomes a helpful hint rather than something to believe in, a trajectory is shifted. We grab a mop, clean up our thinking, and improve things. Paying attention to the connection between what we think and how we feel is a powerful way to become more loving to ourselves and then extend that love and intimacy to others.

~~~~~

When you realize how perfect everything is
you will tilt your head back and laugh at the sky.
—Buddha

8

Do Other People Need Fixing?

ACTOR AND COMEDIAN Martin Mull said, "Having a family is like having a bowling alley installed in your head." Being in an intimate relationship is similar. Partners question, protest, and object. They throw monkey wrenches into our day. They force us to reconsider what we've always done, how we've always been. But this doesn't mean our partner needs fixing.

There's nothing wrong—at all—with your husband (number three) sitting across the breakfast table. Not one thing. He did what he did, said what he said, thought what he thought, and now you're all heated up about it. Nothing is broken, nothing needs fixing, in either one of you. This morning's conversation reveals where you stand personally, though, and that's valuable information. It's also a snapshot of where your connection with each other is stationed.

If you're angry with him, that's not-you. It doesn't mean you should suppress your anger or that being angry is a bad thing. It doesn't mean you're wrong for feeling angry. It means you're expressing a reaction you learned. If you wish to discover true-you, abandon your well-worn path. Singer Fiona Apple's 2020 album advises us to "Fetch the Bolt Cutters." Cut yourself loose from what you've always done. This time, recognize and then set aside evaluation (the rightness or wrongness) of what your partner did. Do your best to set aside the accompanying emotions as well. Don't go down that rabbit hole. It won't help either of you. Get quiet and observe. State facts only. Then, look to see what his words or actions trigger in you. Heal that.

This is the phenomenon spoken about in chapter 1, that a "third something" is created when two people relate. My words were "It's not so much a thing but more of an advantage and a possibility." What opens to you by relating to him is the opportunity to fetch the bolt cutters and release not-you. This tiny moment is revolutionary if you turn your attention to what it would take to heal the hot spot and approach your companion in love instead of reproach. (We'll talk more about how to restore ourselves in Part Three: The Five Core Skills for Making Changes.) Stating a message clearly and without anger gives the best chance of being heard, plus it beckons the most evolved parts of our brain to come up with alternatives. When our mind is calm, creative solutions show themselves.

For now, know that any time you're triggered by someone else, that person has done you a mighty favor. They prodded a place in you that is both tender and misinformed. You can mend that place, and when you do, you'll speak from true-you. True-you summons true-him. And right there is the powerful ripple effect of being yourself. Mahatma Gandhi said, "In a gentle way, you can shake the world."

An Unexpected Lesson

One evening while I was shopping in the Italian food section of my local grocery store, a child a few aisles away was having a loud tantrum. Just as the extra-loud part revved up, a raggedy-looking grandma passed by me pushing her cart. She wore a frumpy sweater and odd-looking pants and walked with a slight limp. She seemed weary. She had heard this child (as had everyone else in the store) and commented to me as she passed, "Somebody oughta just whup that child and teach him a thing or two."

You know how a whole lot can go through your mind in a few quick seconds, including detailed visuals? I wondered what it must have been like to be a child in her home. To imagine her tempestuous history produced stress in my body. My Inner Guidance kicked in to tell me I had begun to manufacture an unfavorable story that would cost my well-being—it hurt to think what I was thinking. Wasn't it good of my faithful guidance system to issue a reminder that my stressful opinions about Grandma would not help me, or her, or those already-whupped children in any way?

After she walked on, I was silent. But we made direct eye contact, and she knew I had heard her. My way of finding center (Love) is to get quiet. So, I got quiet. No need for both of us to be in pain! This grandma made me aware of a truth: thinking unloving thoughts is like giving yourself a good whuppin'.

Silently, I said a thank-you prayer right there in the grocery store, holding the tomato basil sauce that had not yet made it into my cart. This unlikely angel reminded me to be gentle with myself. What a gift from this soul! There was nothing about either one of us that needed fixing. Together, we created a positive ripple.

Something You're Already Good At

Your earthly body is designed for flexibility. Your legs and arms move in all directions. Your eyes, heart, and digestive system support you through motion. The heart pumps, lungs breathe, and legs carry. Even at rest, you shift and evolve. You're a walking miracle.

Researchers have learned plenty about our brainy flexibility, particularly in the field of neuroplasticity, which is the study of the brain's ability to reorganize itself by forming new neural connections in response to unfamiliar situations. Each of our senses—taste, touch, sight, smell, hearing, and balance—uses receptor cells to detect energy. When stimulated, these cells send electrical signals by way of a nerve to a specific area of the brain. For many years, scientists had no idea that areas of the brain were interchangeable. But now they have clear evidence for adaptability, or what is known in the field as "sensory substitution."

Researcher Paul Bach-y-Rita speaks five languages and has lived in six countries. He's an expert in a number of fields, including medicine, psychopharmacology, and biomedical engineering. His studies have included the nervous system, sight, and eye muscles. He asks out-of-the-box research questions such as "Are eyes necessary for seeing?" Bach-y-Rita contends that we don't see with our eyes but rather with our brain.[9] He has concluded that how a sensation enters the brain is less important than how the brain learns to read it.

To apply Bach-y-Rita's decoding concept loosely suggests that an event is less important than how we evaluate the experience. It's not so much about words being said but how the receiver translates them and what is concluded. Author Viktor Frankl, a holocaust survivor, is credited as saying "Between stimulus and response, there is a space. In that space is our power to choose our response. In our response lies our growth and our freedom."

The way we interpret a partner's actions makes a difference. This dances squarely in the face of what we so often believe or practice. If you care about the quality of how you relate, choose interpretations that bless you both.

My response to the grumpy grandma could have been disgust or annoyance. Or I could have dismissed her comment and thought nothing of it. But none of those responses would have blessed us both. My Inner Being gave me guidance, and I listened. How intimate, how loving to be encouraged to open one's field of interpretive possibilities and be in discovery. Tibetan Buddhist meditation master Chögyam Trungpa Rinpoche once remarked, "Openness is like the wind. If you open your doors and windows, it is bound to come in." The guidance of our Inner Being throws open the sashes that frame our old ways, leaving us to realize there is more. There is a higher, more open love.

Let's say you decide to give attention to interpretation, and through open-minded inquiry you discover that your mate wasn't doing what you thought he was doing. In fact, his actions were in your favor and you missed it at first. But with your intelligence aimed toward the identification of a beneficial interpretation, one becomes obvious. Why? Because we tend to find the evidence we're looking for. Love waits for your petition, your prayer. When you give your attention and your voice to love, reasons for loving shake off what covers them.

Fear Not

Marie Monfils, head of the Monfils Fear Memory Lab at the University of Texas in Austin, reported that until recently most psychologists believed that memories, including fear memories, become consolidated (fixed, unchangeable) soon after the memories are acquired. But newer research shows that each time we recall a memory, we can reinterpret it. When we're able to add new information to an old memory, our experience of that memory changes. Her work demonstrates that we can actually turn a fearful memory into a fearless one.[10]

Solo climber Alex Honnold, whose nickname is No Big Deal, is the first (and only) person to date to reach the top of Yosemite's vertical granite rock formation, El Capitan, without the use of ropes or other safety gear. His ascent of the El Cap route known as Freerider is chronicled in the 2018 documentary *Free Solo*.

Veteran explorer Mark Synnott, writing about Honnold's feat for *National Geographic*, says:

> He ascended the peak in 3 hours, 56 minutes, taking the final moderate pitch at a near run. At 9:28 a.m. PDT, under a blue sky and few wisps of cloud, he pulled his body over the rocky lip of summit and stood on a sandy ledge the size of a child's bedroom.[11]

For some of us, simply reading details about his climb increases our respiration or heart rate. Honnold, who has trained himself to have less fear in life-or-death situations, has an amygdala (the part of the brain that regulates emotions and encodes memories) that doesn't fire in the face of danger as it does for most people. In fact, in the face of danger, his amygdala shows no activity at all.

> "With free-soloing, obviously I know that I'm in danger, but feeling fearful while I'm up there is not helping me in any way," he [Honnold] said. "It's only hindering my performance, so I just set it aside and leave it be."[12]

We have interpretive choices. Through practice, we can train our brain not to run us ragged when a serene focus is needed. Mark Synnott writes further about Honnold's practice to maintain calm during a climb:

But the true test for Honnold was whether he could maintain his composure alone on a cliff face hundreds or thousands of feet up while executing intricate climbing sequences where positioning a foot slightly too low or high could mean the difference between life and death. Elite climbers have pointed to Honnold's unique ability to remain calm and analytical in such dangerous situations, a skill that Honnold has slowly developed over the 20 years he has been climbing. [13]

To imagine a negative story about a limping grandma's past is an example of thoughts going rogue. Was I in danger of dying as a result? Thankfully, no. But runaway thoughts of danger would have a profound effect on Honnold dangling midair on the face of a cliff and would more than likely cost him his life.

One last note about Honnold's trip up the granite wall: Did his climb require practice? You bet.

"Years ago, when I first mentally mapped out what it would mean to free solo Freerider, there were half a dozen of pitches where I was like, 'Oh that's a scary move and that's a really scary sequence, and that little slab, and that traverse,'" Honnold said. "There were so many little sections where I thought 'Ughh—cringe.' But in the years since, I've pushed my comfort zone and made it bigger and bigger until these objectives that seemed totally crazy eventually fell within the realm of the possible."[14]

More About the Wonders of Flexibility

Flexibility is powerful. If one career falls apart, we find a new one. If one creative idea crashes and burns, we stir the ashes until another rises, and it might even be better than the first. When one bubble bursts— and it will—along comes another. If we throw ourselves headlong into a romantic endeavor and yet our partner leaves, we recover as best we can and move on.

If you feel stuck in an uncomfortable interpretation of your mate's behavior, one that causes an adverse reaction in you, engage your supple thinking. Ask yourself, "What else could it be?" Think outside your box. Find at least three other perspectives and try them on. Do it for the enjoyment of discovery, and continue until you find an interpretation that relaxes you even slightly.

Assistance from another person can help you focus on your nimble thinking. If you are struggling with your weight, a workout coach, yoga class, or even a phone app can guide you toward a lighter, stronger, healthier you. If your wardrobe needs an update, a personal shopper can help you match your new outlook. Your situation changes, because—flexibility.

Stop the Presses!

Life evolves and expands each time we reinvent ourselves physically, mentally, or emotionally. I did this many times, in many ways with Eric. In particular, the use of the phrase "stop the presses" helped me toss my habit of giving attention to untruths. Imagine a scene where newspapers are being printed, many per hour, on machines with a steady heartbeat. The papers land in a crisp pile at the end of an assembly line. Suddenly a person yells over the loudspeaker, "Stop the presses!" There's an error that can't be published, and the operation is called to a halt.

"Stop the presses" prompted me to pull the giant lever in my mind and go quiet. This is one way I learned to interrupt unloving thoughts. As often as possible, I said the phrase aloud, because giving voice to words is potent. You can do this, too. Reach for the lever. Make it stop. Call it off.

You'll notice something outstanding about the lever: it prevents a battle with the thought. The thought is simply recognized for being untrue, and attention to it is cut off. To pull the lever returns us to the space of simply being. We're smarter when we're calm.

The Fight that Changed Everything

While I'm not proud of the following incident, I'm willing to tell it in order to help you. In 2005, immediately following the mind-shattering "are you done with me" question from Eric, I heeded the advice of Will Rogers, who said, "If you find yourself in a hole, stop digging." I fired myself as a relationship coach in order to restore and reevaluate. Taking time to reappraise my relationship skills is similar to a tennis player who hires a coach to assess her serve and her mindset. It requires humility, courage, and a willingness to set aside what we've learned in favor of discovery, reinvention, and improvement. I was committed to every bit of that.

Eric and I never argued with yells and screams. Instead, when peeved about something, we fumed silently and walked away from each other. But one Friday evening, we broke the quiet rule and got loud. More accurately, I did.

During my self-imposed career intermission, my daily gig was to design closets, garages, entertainment systems, and pantries for residences. This required a visit to the customer's home to measure spaces and produce designs. I was a top seller. My paycheck was commission only.

One week, the company assigned me a customer who caused me to struggle. The commission from her $20,000 job would certainly be a welcome addition to my paycheck, but things weren't easy with this customer. Design adjustments helped accommodate her budget requests, yet nothing seemed good enough for her.

At the time I worked from home, and so did Eric. Unbeknownst to me, he watched and listened as he passed my office on the way to his and witnessed my attempts to please this woman. He saw that I was thoroughly worn out and had begun to grovel, undersell myself, and apologize. He couldn't bear it, but I didn't know. It turns out I wasn't paying attention.

One Friday evening, I called her to finalize her designs, yet she still wasn't satisfied. During our phone conversation, Eric walked up to my desk and said quite loudly, "You don't need this woman. Tell her to take a hike." His bold words took me by surprise, and not in a good way.

Because Eric leaned into the phone and spoke with intention and volume, my customer heard his words plain as day. She said sharply, "Excuse me, who is that talking in the background?" In shock, I replied, "It's my husband." Then, without skipping a beat, he leaned into the phone a second time and repeated himself with more emphasis on specifics. He told her off. I was horrified.

My customer lit into me. Why would anyone, she demanded, especially my husband, interfere with our business? She wondered what kind of a woman would allow such a thing. She hung up, and that was that. The job was gone, along with a fine camera I'd left on the site and had intended to retrieve. I was livid.

I leaped out of my chair, yelled at Eric, and pounded on his chest. (As I said, I'm not proud of my actions, but if telling this story will help anyone, I'm game.) I'm not that strong, and I didn't hurt him, but still, I wanted to hurt him. He never hit back, and neither did he run. He stood solid as a rock, deflecting my sloppiest blows quite gently with his hands. He was not the least bit afraid or even bothered by my tantrum. But I was troubled. Fighting physically with each other had never occurred between us, and now I was the one who blew my fuse. My tirade went on for a while.

Once calm, I couldn't speak to him or look into his eyes, but especially, I couldn't face myself. What had I just done? We said not one word to each other for the rest of the evening and slept with our backs to each other. I couldn't bear the sight of him and couldn't imagine how to forgive him. The question underneath, though, was what would it take to forgive myself? What had made me fly out of control and turn into a madwoman? Even though it was a relief to blow my top, it felt horrible to get physical.

As fate would have it, my schedule included attending a self-help seminar early the next morning where a favorable approach to men would be presented. Seeing Eric in a positive light was the last thing I wanted to do. Plus, how would I deal with my self-criticism about clobbering him? Even one incoming missile of negativity about me would seem excessive. I had nuked myself already.

This incident occurred within a few weeks of my declaration and commitment to turn our marriage around—of course it did! Departing the next morning to drive to the seminar, I was relieved that Eric was still asleep. The note I left on his bedside table let him know that I had no clue why he'd sent my closet customer running but hoped to find out.

Where's the Good?

The next two days focused on men were life-changing. The incident with Eric had certainly primed me to hold everything I thought I knew up to the light. And yes, by scaring off my closet customer, Eric was indeed attempting to do some good. Can you guess what it was? I'll answer this, but first a reminder about my emotional state leading to the meltdown. My stance with this customer was off-kilter. True-me would have given this closet job the boot. I had done it before, many times.

Have you figured out what good thing Eric was trying to do? He was trying to protect me. From what? From whatever was destroying my confidence. He was protecting me from how I treated myself around this customer. Eric wanted me to bend less. If serving a customer meant twisting myself into a knot, and still those efforts weren't enough, then he figured this called for saying goodbye and good luck to the woman who needed closets. The gospel according to Eric was that I should not help her to the detriment of myself.

Well now! Isn't that a loud shot of love? This doesn't mean that Eric was right about what he did with my customer, or that he was wrong. He did what he did. On one hand, he snatched away my chance to work things out with her. We could evaluate his actions as disrespectful, invasive, and entirely out of line. We could say he disregarded my choices in the matter. We could say he owed me an apology.

There were positive options available to both of us that neither of us took. He could have observed the situation and then talked to me before (or after) any negotiation with my customer. I could have initiated a discussion with Eric about my difficulties and asked for his input. Staff members at my company would gladly have assisted had I requested it.

But the point here is that *this is what happened*. This is how the situation unfolded. Given that we each did what we did, how could we best handle it? In one way, I was being too flexible, too accommodating. Yet at the core of the matter was my inflexibility: sell this job no matter what. Eric figured that if I wouldn't save myself from extended stress, then he would save me.

Eric didn't think. He reacted. He did what a man who loves a woman might instinctively do. He took his bow and arrow and killed the threat to my confidence with a quick, clean shot. Well, two shots actually, because he leaned into the phone twice and gave my customer a double dose! His snap reaction saved me from further attempts to please someone who apparently couldn't be pleased. He also saved me from the tiger called myself. He put me and the customer out of misery with great efficiency.

What I'd never acknowledged until that fight was that Eric had no hesitation to step in when I neglected to take care of myself. It's not that I'm helpless. I'd eventually figure things out, but he saved me time. However, if I consider Eric's actions to be interference (which I did at first, and it made me mad as a hornet), or if I think he's trying to control me (which I did at first, and it made me mad as a hornet), then his attempts to contribute are thwarted (as long as I'm mad as a hornet). Nobody wins when I'm mad as a hornet.

Eric was trying to do something *for me,* which I read as *against me.* Were there better ways for him to support me? No doubt he could have used some coaching around this. But in truth, both of us had much to learn. On my side, not only had I neglected to take good care of myself (stop trying so hard) or take care of my customer (let her find a closet company that worked for her), I had also failed to consider the foundation for Eric's actions. He loved me and intended to do good on my behalf.

Dissolve Versus Resolve

In an attempt to resolve conflicts, we often resort to tactics that help us get our way. We label our partner as inconsiderate or rude, for instance, perhaps hoping they'll feel bad enough to drop the behaviors that cause us hurt, embarrassment, or inconvenience. In the fight Eric and I had (i.e. The Fight That Changed Everything), it would be easy to label what he did (he interfered inappropriately), or what I did (I was out of control). In my experience, though, labels used during upsets usually imply a wrongdoing, or occur as a reprimand, which tends to prolong a difficulty. Labeling someone as codependent or toxic doesn't make trouble go away. Instead, it adds importance, weight, and possible self-judgment. Negative assessments of ourselves or others lead to longer recovery times.

Most of us were brought up to think that in a conflict, the end goal is resolution. Resolution means the conflict is over. It implies that the opposing positions or perspectives still exist, but the parties have compromised and a peace treaty has been signed. My preference around solving conflicts is different from resolution. *Dissolving* an issue means that opposing perspectives wash away like sand after a wave. There is no lingering, resigned sense of "Okay, we're not in conflict any more, but I still think my position was valid."

To dissolve a situation so cleanly that it's as if the difficulty never occurred requires a profound commitment to "what if nobody's wrong." Forgiveness becomes unnecessary, because what was thought to have happened didn't. To begin, we say: This is what occurred. (State facts only.) Then we ask: Given that nobody's wrong, how shall we dissolve this? We play with options and consider points of view that bless both people.

When nobody's wrong, nobody feels bad, but it doesn't mean there are no apologies. Eric and I were quick to say "I'm sorry" to each other on many occasions, because it felt natural to do so. In this situation, I don't remember if Eric ever apologized. I do vividly recall that things were settled inside myself so completely that to ask (or expect) him to apologize never occurred to me.

To this day, what remains prominent in my experience is the moment in our conversation when he realized he was trying to do good on my behalf and then forgave himself for stepping in. What happened on his face, with his posture, and within his heart touched me to my core. When his feeling of being wrong dissolved, the mistake disappeared. It was as if time reversed, and the incident had never occurred for either of us. When a person feels honored for the value of his or her contribution, even if that contribution brought trouble initially, the entire matter disappears. Positive finds its feet, and fast.

Because of this fight, I learned to let my inner compass point me toward truth (let a customer go), welcome the consequences (no commission), and direct my efforts toward customers who intended to buy closets. My resolution also involved being more conscious of how my actions with customers *felt*. Instead of living in stress, I could find my way to ease. This new awareness supported my health and well-being, as well as my customers'.

On Eric's side of things, he had jumped into my business and regretted it. My recognition of his attempt to do something good allowed him the grace to forgive himself and, in the future, to leave me to my customers. After all, he preferred to support and empower me, and going forward he did exactly that.

This fight between us was unusual. First, nothing like it had ever happened before, and second, neither did it happen again. We found it unnecessary to repeat the scene, which demonstrates the beauty of "what if nobody's wrong." The upset is done and over with. The only remainders are love and more love.

Since then, many women I've worked with have transformed their experience of events they thought were surely against them but turned out to be quite the opposite. Their anger or resentment gave way to a kinder view of their partners and themselves. As for the men in these sessions? They reinterpreted the situation, too, and granted themselves credit where credit was due. They recovered self-respect and confidence, and sometimes they wept. Both partners were more loving when all was said and done.

For Eric, my regard for myself was more important than time spent or a commission earned. For me, I was in deep with this project (sell the closets no matter what) and intended to make my investment worth something. It's a funny thing we do: if we're paid enough for being in hell, we can justify having gone there. But, thankfully, with two swift swings of his verbal machete, Eric saved me from my determination to make hell worth it. He sliced the problem out of my life and left me to figure out what to do next. How efficient. How loving.

This experience informed my awareness in a pivotal way. How many times had he done something on my behalf, and I totally missed it? And how many times had I pushed past my Inner Guidance—ignored it? Because of this incident, our capacity to love and understand each other grew like green grass after a spring rainstorm. It was especially satisfying to keep the commitment to myself that no matter what problem or difference arose between us, we would come out the other side in love.

~~~~~

To be fully seen by somebody, then, and be loved anyhow—
this is a human offering that can border on miraculous.
—Elizabeth Gilbert

Life
is
in favor
of me.

9

Life Favors You

THE POET RUMI is credited with the words "Live life as if everything is rigged in your favor." My daughter's dog, Baguette, a Lab mix, lives as Rumi suggests. Baguette assumes any dog she meets is a playmate.

My beloved Jackson, an eleven-pound rescue who passed away in 2020, was a long-haired Chihuahua, aggressive around other dogs. He didn't enjoy being combed, having his nails clipped, or meeting small children, either. A pet-sitter friend with six small dogs of her own offered to help Jackson learn to play nicely with others. We gave Jackson a test, or more accurately, a pup quiz. She said it was important that no dog be on a leash, but just in case things went awry, her husband stood poised with a water hose to break up a fight.

After Jackson acclimated to her yard, she let her dogs out of the house. They headed toward him in a friendly pack, happy tails wagging. Jackson was overwhelmed. He sat down and fell completely still. Gradually, though, he found his nerve. He interacted with them defensively at first, then offensively, and finally he let them know they should leave him alone, which they did.

Back to Baguette

Up to this point, my daughter and I had mostly kept our dogs apart because it was a lot of work to have them in the same space. But after

Jackson's encounter with six small dogs, I wondered how he might do with medium-size, happy-go-lucky Baguette. We scheduled an outdoor rendezvous at my house in the country, which gave a safe run of things without leashes. If anyone could make things turn out well, Baguette could.

Top dog Baguette was a little surprised at Jackson's style, but she took him in stride. She played his way. Faster and bigger than Jackson, she was able to get out of his way easily, or take a flying leap over him if necessary, which she did once. She dodged his lunges happily and at full tilt. He certainly offered her a new game. The more Jackson pursued, the more Baguette invited it. How brilliant!

Baguette began to imitate Jackson. When he barked, she barked back as if to say, "Oh, so that's how you like it!" When Jackson ran after her, she'd fly away, then do an about-face. This caught him off guard at first, because he didn't interpret her return move as playful, and it threw him into a little more fear. In response, he ran after her again, which is exactly what she was after. Essentially, Baguette welcomed whatever Jackson did and turned it into amusement and joy. She dashed about with full-throttle enthusiasm.

Jackson wore himself out expressing his fear. To run, bark, defend, and pursue required energy, and eventually he slowed. Baguette hunkered down ten feet away and gazed intently while he caught his breath. When he didn't come after her, she barked a happy invitation. When that didn't work she went directly to him, smelled him, and poked gently with her paw to encourage continuation of their game.

Clearly, Baguette is a four-legged master. She never resisted Jackson. She welcomed his actions and turned them into playful exchange. She received him as he was. She didn't manage him. Nor did she reprimand, scare, threaten, or overpower him. She bounded about as if Jackson were the most delightful and fascinating friend she'd ever met.

Eventually, her play and his fear turned into play on both sides. We noticed Jackson's tail wagging happily as he barked. Jackson was thoroughly exhausted after it was over, his fear drawn out of him like a long ribbon. He seemed relaxed, settled, and quietly confident—downright pleased with himself about how things turned out.

Applying Baguette's brilliance to our own lives suggests that we might consider the value of being less serious with others (perhaps partners and ex-partners), that it would be time well spent to interact in ways that bring out tail-wagging on both sides.

So Nice to Have a Friend Who Doesn't Believe in Your Fear

Jackson became a calmer dog after Baguette ran circles around his fear. There was the simple wonder of how she saw him: that Jackson was playing. And so, eventually, he played! Jackson was able to be happier with her than with other dogs. Baguette is evidence that one individual can transform a relationship. Baguette played with Jackson in a way that proved he was friendship-worthy. What a good and fortunate thing to have a friend who doesn't read our actions as a problem. Baguette witnessed Jackson's defensiveness and loved him anyway.

How lucky to have a friend who embraces our anger, as Eric did when I was upset about the loss of my closet customer. He didn't fight me. He let me lunge, bark, and growl until I wore myself out and began to wag my tail. Eric accepted what I did and loved me anyway. In the end I was able to accept Eric, too. Even though we tussled, nobody got hurt, and both of us were all the better for it when it was over.

Kid Games

My daughter was born when I was almost forty years old, and I became a single mother. As time went on, MacKenzie and I talked about how we wished our family were a little larger, that we "needed more people." We set up playdates with friends or got together with other families quite regularly. On this day, two sisters (ages four and five) had joined us for a library outing. Things got testy in the back seat between the sisters, so I found a safe place to stop the car and work things out face-to-face. Turning to Janet [the older], I queried, "Do you know what game you're playing with Dani?" Janet stared at me as if to say, "What an odd question..." and then slowly shook her head. "No."

~~~~~

Note: Brief commentary intended to guide and inform is in italics and indented, like this.

Me: Can you figure out what this game is? How do you play it? Can you teach me?

Janet: I don't know what you mean.

Me: A game has players...and equipment...and rules. Right? You're playing a game with Dani and there's a doll. Tell me about the doll.

Janet: Well, I have the doll.

Dani [the younger sister]: And all her clothes. I want to hold her.

Me: The doll and her clothes are the equipment. [We talk about how this compares to equipment in basketball or football.] Then what happens in this game?

Janet: She's trying to take the doll from me.

Me: Yes! You're doing so well describing this! Does this game have rules?

Janet: I want the doll. It's mine.

Dani: But I want the doll, too, and I want to change her outfit.

Me: So the game is...Janet has the doll and clothes, and she's not letting anyone else have any of it, no matter what! Right?

> *The light goes on in Dani's head. She's the younger one, yet comprehends the game idea first. Janet notices Dani's delight and seems curious about why Dani is suddenly sunny.*

Me [to Janet]: So the game is that you're keeping the doll away from others. Dani is trying to get the doll from you. Go ahead, Dani! Try to get Janet to give you the doll.

Dani [laughing while trying to act tough]: You better give me that doll right now or I'm going to bop you on the head!

In response, Janet smiles playfully and holds on to the doll even tighter. She begins to see the game.

Me: Dani, did it work? Did you get the doll?

Dani [totally delighted, throws her hands up]: Nope!

Me: So, Dani, what else will you try—without hurting Janet—'cause I'm the referee and if you hurt her, I'll throw you out of the game.

I'm dramatic and full of laughter, but as tough as Dani was a few seconds ago.

Me: That's what referees do, don't they? They call a foul, and throw a flag. Hey, I need a whistle! Anybody got a whistle?

Dani shows me she can whistle—pretty impressive!

Me: Dani, can I hire you? [She lights up and says yes.] So when I point to you, you whistle for me, okay? This pays big bucks, you know.

Dani's got chutzpah, and she tells me to pay her a million dollars for being her whistler. We discuss her proposal.

Me: All right, anybody have a name for this game yet?

MacKenzie [my daughter, who's been silent so far]: "Keep the Doll."

Me: That name would work, wouldn't it? Any other ideas?

Nobody's got any, 'cause this idea of turning an argument into a delightful game is new and weird.

Me: Yes! The game could be called Keep the Doll or Keep Away. There's a prize—the doll and her clothes—and you keep it away from everyone else.

~~~~~

Back at home, we played versions of Keep Away where two were allowed to team up against the third to compete for a coveted prize. At one point they resorted to surprise attacks at random during the day, all in good fun. After that we explored names for games when there was a struggle. We played like Baguette and Jackson, to make what was once a difficulty (aggressiveness for Jackson or not sharing for Janet) the centerpiece of positive play.

Grownups Play Grown-Up Games

There were times during a spat with Eric where I'd say, "You know, look at us. What are we doing? Well, actually, what am I doing? I'm resisting your attempt to convince me that the world is going to hell in a handbasket because of the awful people in the government. There's no need for me to resist." Once calm, my tune changed. "What else do you want to tell me? I'm all ears."

Asking him questions wasn't for the purpose of appeasement but rather to give my flexible nature a workout. In so doing, I learned. About him. About me. About us. My frustration became an exploratory conversation instead of a fight. I became Baguette: "Okay, Eric, you want to play with opinions? Let's play that way." To play like Baguette made it easier for the defensive part of me to learn leash-free on a friendlier playground.

How About Dessert?

Chef Massimo Bottura, famous for creating nontraditional Italian food, tells a story about his restaurant, Osteria Francescana, in Modena, Italy. The restaurant has twelve tables, three Michelin stars, and a stunning collection of contemporary art. One of the restaurant's signature desserts came about in an unusual way. While preparing a lemon tart, pastry chef Kondo Takahiko accidentally dropped it and it broke. Rather than trash it and start over, he turned the smashed tart into a work of art. Now they drop the tarts on purpose. Tweezers are used to place some of the tastes (salty capers, candied bergamot, lemongrass, and mint sauce) in artistic patterns. The now famous dessert, Oops, I Dropped a Lemon Tart, is featured in Massimo Bottura's cookbook *Never Trust a Skinny Italian Chef.*

If a situation appears to take a turn for the worse, ask: "What if this disaster is actually helping me? How could this crazy mistake be a good thing?" The slow traffic in front of you might be saving your life. Or you're in a rush and late for a meeting, and unbeknownst to you the person you're to meet is late also. What if the universe is offering you a chance to relax while simultaneous arrivals are orchestrated? Life is too short to go nuts about things that don't matter in the long run. You will not care on your deathbed about a broken lemon tart or lateness to a meeting.

Life can be *for us* in ways we might not expect, including that it might be the right time to leave our relationship. A helping hand has two sides: move on and stay. Trust the wisdom that is shown to you. Don't worry. Love never leaves, even when relationships come and go. Sometimes it's truly best to start over.

It is often said that things work out best for those who make the best of how things work out. If we believe life is for us, this is the idea we feed. It becomes the lens through which we view our day. We can keep a perspective, tweak it, or trade it in. Feel free to make creative adjustments as you go. Know that life favors you.

~~~~~

Heaven goes by favor. If it went by merit, you
would stay out and your dog would go in.
—Mark Twain

Close your eyes, fall in love.
Stay there.

—Rumi

PART TWO

Getting Along with the Opposite Sex

10

Why Not Start with Sex

ACTRESS KATHARINE HEPBURN said, "Sometimes I wonder if men and women really suit each other. Perhaps they should live next door and just visit now and then." To be attuned to your partner involves the challenge of including another, often opposite, reality. Education that opens our perspective makes a difference—sometimes *the difference*—in our ability to achieve harmony in the presence of so many contrasts.

To that end, this section is an exploration of distinctions. It's an important prelude to the five core skills in part three, and to the conversations with clients. This material turned some beliefs of mine upside down in a way that grew my compassion and helped me help us cooperate in places we'd been struggling. Entire books have been written about the impact of male-female differences, so consider this an appetizer version of a comprehensive subject.

We'll begin this section with a brief mention of males and females as sexual beings. Since human beings are fundamentally social, sex with another person is one way to share a meaningful bond. The desire to maintain a close physical connection can be a powerful reason to get along with someone we love. Then comes an exploration of the dance between masculine and feminine, followed by the influence of our Survival Selves. For dessert, there's a client conversation to illustrate key concepts.

It's to your advantage to approach this information without prejudice. If you apply the filter "I agree or disagree," you'll miss the value of what's presented. It's impossible to learn anything new when we're only looking to validate and reinforce our current point of view.

Male-Female

Most complex animals, including humans, have two sexes. Male is defined as the physiological sex that produces sperm. Females, on the other hand, bear offspring and/or produce eggs. In human males and females, hormones guide our actions. Although male bodies are quite different from female bodies, it has taken science and medicine time to fully acknowledge this. For much of the twentieth century, scientists assumed that women were essentially small men. According to neuropsychiatrist, researcher, and clinician Dr. Louann Brizendine, by the 1970s and '80s, it had already been discovered that male and female animal brains develop differently in utero. Despite this, medical students were taught that humans express sex differences primarily from the influences of environment and upbringing.

Until eight weeks old, a fetal human brain is female. But after that, the brain begins to change according to genes and sex hormones. A surge in testosterone at eight weeks kills off cells in communication centers and grows more cells in the sex, muscular action, and aggression centers. Without incoming testosterone, the brain continues to develop as female. Brain development influences how we see the world and how we engage with it. Even though male and female brain circuits are similar, they use different pathways to accomplish the same task.

In females, more fully developed communication and emotion centers in the brain allow a girl baby to read faces, connect emotionally, and be more talkative than her brothers. This was originally interpreted by researchers as girls being needier than boys, but is now read as girls being more mature at birth than boys. The parallel for male babies is their interest in and ability to investigate objects in the environment (boys disassembling toys to learn about them, for example).

Males have a higher sex drive than most females, which can prompt other interpretive biases. According to Dr. Brizendine, the sexual pursuit area in the male brain is about 2.5 times larger than the same area in females.

> ...beginning in their teens, they produce 20 to 25-fold more testosterone than they did during pre-adolescence. If testosterone were beer, a 9-year-old boy would be getting the equivalent of a cup a day. But a 15-year-old would be getting the equivalent of nearly two gallons a day. This fuels their sexual engines and makes it impossible for them to stop thinking about female body parts and sex.[15]

Jokes are made about how the true male brain exists below his belt. However, this doesn't begin to represent who men are or the brain changes they experience as they move through the stages of their life. From Dr. Brizendine:

> There are also the seek-and-pursue baby-boy brain, the must-move-or-I-will-die toddler brain; the sleep-deprived, deeply bored, risk-taking teen brain; the passionately bonded mating brain; the besotted daddy brain; the obsessed-with-hierarchy aggressive brain; and the fix-it-fast emotional brain. In reality, the male brain is a lean, mean problem-solving machine.[16]

Foreplay, Adventure, and Orgasms

Sex between males and females involves quite a few opposites.

- For both sexes, the amygdala (fear, anxiety, worry, self-consciousness center of the brain) must be deactivated in order to climax. After that, for males it's a simple matter of hydraulics (blood rushing to one main location) and orgasm control, specifically to be able to delay them. For her to have successful sex (including but not limited to her climax), giving up control is necessary. It also takes her longer to deactivate her amygdala.

- Sex therapists often say that for females, foreplay is everything that happens in the twenty-four hours preceding intercourse, but for males, foreplay is the three minutes before entry.
- Males tend to be sexually more adventurous than females, according to a national study by Dr. Edward Laumann[17], and males actively seek regular sex. Females are more likely to say that desire for sex centers around open communication or the right circumstances.
- More than 90 percent of males experience orgasm during intercourse.[18] Only about 25–50 percent of females do. (Research numbers vary greatly and hinge on many factors. It's complicated.)[19]

You're a sexual being. You deserve intimacy, pleasure, and connection—good sex is good for true-you. It helps us live a healthier life and contributes to a sense of calm, inner peace, and satisfaction. In the words of speaker and author Marianne Williamson[20], "Some men know that a light touch of the tongue, running from a woman's toes to her ears, lingering in the softest way possible in various places in between, given often enough and sincerely enough, would add immeasurably to world peace."

I hope you've enjoyed this appetizer. Next, have a seat at the table. Take a moment to rearrange your silverware and have a sip of water. Here comes the soup.

~~~~~

"Since you dismissed your maid," he said,
"I suppose it will be up to me to undress you."
"That is most chivalrous of you, my lord."
—Julianne MacLean, *Love According to Lily*

11

Created Equal Doesn't Mean Created Identical

MY DEEPEST HOPE has been that all people on Earth might one day walk with one another as equals, and accept and love one another. Harmony has been on my wish list for as long as I can remember. You might imagine how unsettling it was for me to have a dream of unity yet be unable to create long-lasting cooperation with three of my husbands. My education, creativity, and strong desire for accord were not enough to maintain my intimate relationships. My thoughts turned to other well-educated, well-intentioned, spirited individuals who dreamed of thriving partnerships. Did we all have something in common? How was it possible that so many smart, resourceful humans couldn't live with a partner in peace?

The purpose of this chapter is to help you make love work. It includes some details about getting along that you may never have considered. We'll gather up aspects of you—parts you treasure and parts you may have shunned—and invite them back into whole you. To say to these parts, "Come home." The idea is that if you can partner kindly with all of your qualities, you can partner with anyone. We begin with the question "How do the Masculine Principle and the Feminine Principle work in tandem within me?"

The Visual

Imagine the Masculine Principle as a vertical idea. Up-down, top-bottom. Head is high, feet grounded. The power of the Masculine Principle lies in the ability to be singular, focused, and oriented in this moment, the now.

Imagine the Feminine Principle as a horizontal idea that extends out over an eternal horizon. The power of the Feminine Principle lies in the ability to be inclusive, flexible, and timeless. It includes the past and the not-yet-born future.

Picture these vertical and horizontal ideas as moving, translucent sheets within each of us. Where and how these masculine and feminine sheets meet is different within each person. Individuals express a one-of-a-kind, light-filled blend of masculine and feminine.

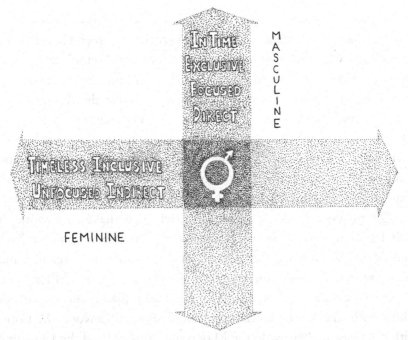

Masculine and Feminine Traits
Illustration by David Cohen

Women can tend toward masculine, just as men can tend toward feminine. Some girl babies arrive as delicate little flowers, others as tomboys. A woman connects to her masculine aspects as she works toward a goal, completes a task, or brings a vision into physical reality. Some men are born with a softer side, while others access it through meditation, creativity, or learning to move with the flow. They also learn it by being around women.

Because each of us has a unique mingling of masculine and feminine, to describe women as only feminine or to describe men as only masculine is inadequate. A woman in the (feminine) flow who sees her child in danger snaps her (masculine) focus into place to ensure the child's safety. Having access to her blend of the masculine-feminine spectrum forwards the brilliance of her body and mind exactly when and how she needs it. The same idea is true for men. They actualize by including their broadest possible expression of both masculine and feminine.

Each item listed under "Feminine Principle" and under "Masculine Principle" represents an advantageous quality. This cannot be emphasized enough. Only by reading each quality as beneficial is it possible to comprehend their united value. Rather than explore *whether* someone's masculine or feminine influence is positive, we ask, *how* is it positive? This also helps us realize the good in our own actions. We drop the query "Did I do the right thing?" and instead ask, "What was good *in* what I did? What's good *about* it? How can I create good *as a result* of it?"

A person coming mostly from the Feminine Principle will be referred to as a feminine and called her or she. A person coming predominately from the Masculine Principle will be referred to as a masculine and called him or he. With all this in mind, consider the following descriptions of principles we'll call Feminine and Masculine.

The Principles

Timeless/In Time

The Feminine Principle is timeless: eternal, everlasting, immortal. Time isn't a factor; there is no concern for time. When a feminine person says, "I'll call you in five," she doesn't mean five minutes. She means, "I'll call you shortly" or "as soon as I can within about fifteen minutes" or "pretty soon, when I finish what I'm doing."

The Masculine Principle is based in the present. It means being, existing, or occurring at this time or now; current.

Inclusive/Exclusive

The Feminine Principle is inclusive: all-encompassing and comprehensive. Inclusivity is sweeping and liquid. It has no location. It is not defined by boundaries, containers, rules or regulations, or by limited understanding. A feminine approach to life is contextual and holistic. Pure feminine is space.

The Masculine Principle is exclusive: unshared, sole, restricted or limited to the person, group, or area concerned. This principle represents the power to exclude considerations, events, and existences, and it supports the ability to focus and produce results. The masculine is committed to that which manifests in physical reality.

Indirect/Direct

The Feminine Principle is indirect: not straight. The approach is nonlinear and nonsequential. It is stream of consciousness. Being indirect endorses moves in any direction, without bias. The feminine bypasses logic and reason. The feminine supports inspired innovation.

The Masculine Principle is direct: extending or moving from one place to another by the shortest route without a change in direction or a stop. This approach is linear and sequential. Directness is efficient and employs clear communication and action. Direct individuals make decisions quickly and tend to state personal opinions as facts.

When a feminine uses directness to her advantage, her worldly effectiveness can be accented. Imagine a feminine spiritual leader, for instance, with a team of people to get her message out using current technology. When a masculine accesses untamed intelligence, his brilliance mushrooms. When men and women embody both the masculine and feminine within, they invite all those around them into an expanded version as well.

Diffuse Awareness/Focused Awareness

The Feminine Principle has diffuse awareness: not paying attention to a particular thing, spread out, scattered widely, poured out like a liquid. This fosters panoramic awareness and allows for the balance of multiple ideas, problems, and solutions simultaneously. Utilizing diffuse awareness supports a spacious, unimpeded, free approach to All Possibilities.

The Masculine Principle is focused. This facilitates the accomplishment of outcomes in the least amount of time. Distractions don't derail. Steve Jobs said, "People think focus means saying yes to the thing you've got to focus on. But that's not what it means at all. It means saying NO to the hundred other good ideas that there are."

A focused individual controls the environment to improve productivity and uses tools and technology that best support. A focused person keeps a to-do list and prioritizes items. Gossip is ignored, and the past isn't dwelled upon. Procrastination, multitasking, or making rash decisions aren't viable options. Rest and recovery are planned and deliberate.

More About Approaches

The Feminine Principle includes known and unknown universes; global humanity; plant, insect, and animal kingdoms; our air; all types of bodies of water and moisture systems; everything underground, microorganisms, root systems, soil. The feminine nurtures what nurtures life. She experiences herself as a mother of all. By the way, if you express primarily as feminine, remember to bring your awareness of the nurturing circle back to your personal well-being. Take care of individual you. With a naturally wide scope, a feminine sometimes forgets about herself, because she is naturally oriented to the whole.

The Masculine Principle, on the other hand, begins with him as center and moves outward. His goal-oriented plan includes a commitment to win. A pure masculine's speed of sequential processing has a fast-switch, on-off feeling around it. Feminine multitasking is invisible and feels like music.

The sacred masculine is a blend of masculine and feminine, the unity of head and heart, mind and body. Some examples: honor without a desire for war, or rational thinking without a need to control. The sacred masculine is committed to making evident what the sacred feminine holds as heaven on earth. The sacred feminine is the energy of creation, the gift of life, a powerful and intuitive internal force. Sacred feminine is space and flow. Sacred masculine and sacred feminine work together to support life on earth, all species thriving.

Daily and Practical

Differences in masculine-feminine orientation are illustrated in the following story about a couple heading out on weekend errands. He assumes she knows what she needs and, more specifically, that she has a list (though she may not). For her, errands are a malleable idea, a blank canvas. His natural approach includes preplanned locations and order of stops, but she's at her best when she creates on the fly.

They set out. Once in the car, her attention tunes in more specifically to what she needs. He's the driver today, and she requests stops. Some are a surprise to him, and he adjusts. They happen upon a roadside herb stand, and she's been looking for chives and basil. At the next stop, she stocks up on locally grown produce. Here, a friend of hers shows up, a well-timed delight. They'd been wanting to connect. There are other spontaneous stops as well, and at the end of the morning, she's pleased with their accomplishments, but he's a little unsettled. He had mentally allotted a couple of hours for the excursion, but it turned out to be double. Other things on his agenda didn't get addressed.

With recognition of each other's styles, outings could be more satisfying. He could bring work along or bow out entirely. She could check on his available time and adjust accordingly. They could do certain errands together and others separately. There are so many ways to cooperate when two people take into account their differences.

To understand another person by way of our own beliefs, attitudes, or orientation doesn't actually tell us who that person is. It tells us who we think they are based on what we know about ourselves. For instance, to a feminine type, a masculine approach could seem limited or tedious. To a masculine type, a feminine style might appear scattered or inefficient. It's easy to judge the other sex as a version of ourselves that needs improvement.

But what if nobody's wrong? What if nobody needs fixing?

Men on Women

Here are statements from three men generated at the outset of our work about the ways they became frustrated with women they loved. Following each statement is a short discussion about his point of view.

~~~~~

What he said: "Stop trying to fix me. Did you marry me for what I could become, or were you happy with me as I am? Ten minutes ago you said I'm just right, and now I'm the most imperfect creature that ever existed. I can't handle the switch from 'I love you; you're the best,' to 'What on earth did I ever see in you?'"

Why he said it: He married her—all of her—and that's that. She already passed all of his tests (an example of being focused, direct). He's attracted to her, loves how she is, and hopes she'll stay the same (exclusive).

Some of his stress comes from an assumption that she's similar to him. But she isn't. She didn't marry him hoping he'd stay the same. She's naturally open to change and evolution, even presses for it. The age-old cosmic joke is that he married her hoping she'll stay the same, and she married him hoping he'll change.

~~~~~

What he said: "Why was an occasional pizza, beer, and a game of darts a wonderful evening out while we were dating, and now it's the poorest choice in the world?"

Why he said it: He's confused because "what works" (pizza, beer, and darts on date night) changed. His frame of mind is "Don't mess with what works" (direct, focused). For him, once a win, always a win (exclusive).

~~~~~

What he said: "Can't we just get along?"

Why he said it: He values efficiency (time-focused, exclusive). Cooperation with his wife is worth his time and attention. When she's happy and satisfied, the whole family feels it. Her happiness is a big win, and he's committed to that (focused, direct).

~~~~~

After some education and bridge-building between their way of thinking and feminine reality, these men were able to offer their wives, partners, and girlfriends loving responses rather than pushback. It was a privilege to witness the impact of their changes, especially that no compromise was needed, no dialed-back version of themselves.

Instead, these men learned to aim their skills more precisely. Their strength and confidence about their participation in the partnership grew because they were able to deliver more of what they wanted to offer. For example, by talking things through with his wife, one man found more ways to win and make a difference in their day-to-day life. Rather than assume his accuracy about what mattered most to her, he asked questions. He was able to give what she requested, and she was able to receive it. The tenderness and appreciation between them skyrocketed.

Women on Men

Now for the other side of the coin. The question for women: what frustrates you about the man you love? Here are three examples.

~~~~~

What she said: "My husband tries to fix my problems. Why can't he just listen to me?"

Why she said it: She first addresses a problem by making space for it to exist, not to fix it or get rid of it (inclusive). To share a difficulty with her husband helps her externalize the question at hand, as if the circumstance is not really about her (indirect). Once the predicament is outside her, she can see it more clearly and invent new possibilities. She assumes that listening to her is a simple no-brainer. Surely he knows how! He must be deliberately choosing not to do it.

Note: An upcoming conversation in chapter 24, Two Angry People Find Love Again, speaks more specifically on how to listen to each other.

~~~~~

What she said: "My husband is dismissive and condescending about my shopping and girl time."

Why she said it: Shopping allows her to feel unhurried (timeless) while she spreads attention in all directions over colors, textures, and fragrances (unfocused, inclusive). Not aiming her awareness anywhere in particular relaxes her. Girl time is also talk time, which decants overflowing elation or distress and clears space.

~~~~~

What she said: "Are men superficial? Are they shallow? Why don't they share their feelings when asked?"

Why she said it: Feelings are a valuable guide for her, and she assumes the same is true for him. When he doesn't share his feelings, she concludes that he must be avoiding them and tags him as emotionally unavailable.

But what if that's not true? What if there's more to the story? In fact, emotions don't guide his actions. He values unbiased decisions and sets his emotions aside to focus, compartmentalize, or "do the right thing." Nothing is lacking in him. Nothing is wrong. But because he's doing the opposite of what she does, she is certain that something needs repair.

~~~~~

Again, with some bridge-building, these women grew closer to the men they loved. Rather than dismiss or discount their mate, they shared and problem-solved. The information on emotional differences was especially life-changing for one woman. By adopting an expanded perspective, she found reasons to respect her partner rather than mark his actions as negative. "What if nobody's wrong" allowed her the freedom to discover areas in their relationship where she could broaden her point of view and bring ease and appreciation to their connection.

A Familiar Story

Here's a short story about masculine-feminine differences, one most couples tell me in a session sooner or later. Interestingly, these stories often involve a moving vehicle. One of the simplest variations goes like this.

~~~~~

After a couple of hours on their road trip, a wife turns to her husband and asks, "Are you hungry?" He says "no" and keeps driving. Silence ensues. They arrive at their destination.

HIM [to his wife]: Are you okay? You seem extra quiet.

HER: I'm fine.

HIM: But you stopped talking to me.

HER: Well, actually, I was hungry.

HIM: Why didn't you tell me?

HER: I did tell you.

HIM: No, you didn't.

HER: I most certainly did. I asked if you were hungry.

HIM: What does asking whether *I'm* hungry have to do with *you* being hungry?

HER: I opened the hunger conversation. You shut it down. It would have been nice if you had returned the question.

An exchange follows, and he insists she be more direct: "Say what you mean, please, and ask your real question." She feels criticized and confused when he presses for his solution to prevent this from happening in the future, and their conversation ends in a stalemate.

~~~~~

We can look at this situation as a bystander and suggest easy solutions. But the significance is that this is a place where people get hung up—and often! A feminine reality doesn't begin or end with personal feelings or body sensations. To ask if her husband is hungry is a natural start to a conversation that concerns both of them. Quizzing him is indirect, unfocused, and inclusive.

She doesn't consciously realize there's even another way to be. Neither does he perceive how different they are from one another. If he recognized her inclusivity, he could return the question: "How about you? Are you hungry?" She could also learn to spot when she's being indirect and add a dose of direct instead.

Next is another story with two versions. In the first, the partners don't take advantage of their masculine-feminine differences. In the second story, they do.

Version 1: Less Cooperation

A couple wakes on a sunny Saturday morning. In a few hours, they'll head out on a day trip. She opens her eyes, tunes in to her husband, her three children, and the feel of the day ahead. She hears her youngest child fussing and heads down the hall to check him and his siblings. She comforts the fussing child while her husband and the other two children sleep.

After cleaning and dressing her youngest, she scoops him up, strolls to the kitchen, and opens the door to the deck. With her son in her arms, she breathes in the morning. Content and satisfied, she wanders inside toward the coffeepot and begins the brew. Muffins go into the oven to warm, the cat is fed, and herbs on the kitchen windowsill are watered, all with her son on one hip. She heads back to the other two children now waking and helps them into their outfits. They walk sleepily to the kitchen. The children play contentedly while she begins picnic prep for the day's outing.

Meanwhile, her husband has showered and taken care of business details that will allow him to focus on the day. He enters the kitchen and says, "How can I help?"

She thinks, "Of course you ask now—when most everything is done except for my shower." She's frustrated that she must state her needs. Isn't it o-b-v-i-o-u-s the children need to be cared for and dressed and food packed before the trip?

As he walks into the kitchen, he's centered and ready to assist. He took care of himself so that he would be entirely available to her and is caught off guard by her reaction. He isn't sure how to get a productive conversation started. Asking questions sometimes makes things worse.

~~~~~

Here's the version of the story that includes awareness of masculine-feminine differences. You'll notice they are a cooperative tag team.

Version 2: More Cooperation

The night before, the two chat briefly about preparation for the day trip, and they agree on a plan. In the morning, the husband rises twenty minutes before his wife, showers, and readies himself for the day. He checks the children, finds the youngest one fussing, and comforts, cleans, and dresses him. He scoops him up and takes him to the kitchen while he feeds the cat and starts the coffee.

Meanwhile, his wife wakes up and showers. When she joins her husband, they get the other two children dressed, and the whole family heads to the kitchen.

The husband begins breakfast prep as his wife waters the windowsill herbs. She heads to the deck to get a feel for her day, then joins him in the kitchen. They all sit down for breakfast. After that he takes care of some business details. Once he's back, she attends to texts and emails, and then the two of them finish breakfast cleanup and picnic prep. They load the car. En route to the destination, he reaches for her hand. She smiles and takes it. They are content, each thankful for the contribution of the other as they set out on their adventure.

This is an example of how regard for differences and brief attention to prep the night before sets a cooperative tone for their morning. This couple will grow closer over time because they set themselves up for it. Daily building blocks are respectful. They cultivate kindness and regard for one another, and intimacy grows. Rather than ignore or work against their masculine-feminine differences, they take advantage of them.

~~~~~

Men and women are like right and left hands;
it doesn't make sense not to use both.
—Jeannette Rankin

12

Survival of the Species

NOW THAT WE'VE covered information about sex differences and masculine-feminine principles, next comes the main meal: the powerful influence of our built-in human features. The part of our design responsible for the continuation of the species will be referred to as our Survival Selves, using the sex-specific names CaveMan and CaveWoman. This third set of information is the least familiar to most of us. It is rarely addressed in education, therapy, or even casual conversation yet has profound effects on our interactions. The information comes from a blend of research from three main sources: psychologist and author Dr. Rick Hanson, relationship educator Alison Armstrong, and neuropsychiatrist, researcher, and clinician Dr. Louann Brizendine. It is my intention that the use and acknowledgment of the teachings of others honors them in every way. We stand on the shoulders of all those before us. In my experience, this blended perspective creates breathing room for solutions that bring harmony and peace of mind.

An Overview

According to Dr. Rick Hanson, "To keep our ancestors alive, Mother Nature evolved a brain that routinely tricked them into making three mistakes: overestimating threats, underestimating opportunities, and underestimating resources (for dealing with threats and fulfilling opportunities). This is a great way to pass on gene copies but a lousy way to promote quality of life."[21]

When our Survival Self is activated, it sends a detectable alert. Do you know the basic signal? When a threat is perceived, we feel tension, along with a matching emotion, such as worry, anger, or fear. Educator Alison Armstrong proposes that CaveMan protects and provides. CaveWoman adapts and nurtures. Besides the information in this chapter, you'll get to know more in client conversations later in the book. To begin, here are examples of messages from our Survival Selves that center specifically around safety and reproduction.

Some Comparisons About Safety

On Threats

> **CaveWoman:** She worries about the safety of her college-bound daughter, her race-car-driving husband, and the bad weather coming. She frets in apocalyptic ways. One day, while downloading a new program on my computer, I accidentally granted permission for the installation of two other (undesirable) programs. Panic set in: "Oh no! My computer's going to die, and I'll lose all my data!" It made me laugh to recognize my Survival Self at her doomsday best. There was no harm done. The correction was easy.

> **CaveMan:** During an average day, his focus is not on his own physical safety. He is tuned to notice others who need protection. Where he drives, where he works, or at home with his family, he is aware and ready to lend a hand.

On Being Out of the Cave

> **CaveWoman:** Being safe and protected is a priority, at home or otherwise. In parking lots at night,

CaveWoman scans the environment for signs of danger as you walk to your car. Navigating big-city streets on foot, this Survival Self is the voice that cautions you to be mindful and listen carefully for anything behind you. CaveWoman knows when to stare someone down and when to look away.

CaveMan: Being out of the cave is natural for CaveMan. It puts him in position to gather information and goods to help him protect and provide. My husband and I lived on a mountain with a steep and winding road, and even in oncoming bad weather, he insisted on going out in sleet or snow for items we needed in preparation for an approaching storm. This was his way of "checking the perimeter," as well as bringing home supplies to hold us for a few days, in case we were unable to get out.

On Being Alone

CaveWoman: Her advice is to travel in groups of at least two. According to her, you should also be in a relationship even if the relationship is not great, because the presence of another person protects you. CaveWoman drives you toward being with other people. Odds are it's safer.

CaveMan: He looks out for others in need of help. One day, I stopped at a gas station and noticed that one of my tires was low. A male customer at the station saw my dilemma and asked if he could assist. He discovered a nail in my left front tire and fixed it using a tire repair kit purchased from the station. When I thanked him and offered to pay for the kit and his time, he refused, saying that roadside assistance was his thing. This is modern-day CaveMan, on the lookout and ready to protect and provide.

Some Comparisons About Reproduction

Because all of us have plenty of instincts around sex, being educated about our Survival Selves helps us remember not to turn natural, built-in urges into reasons to criticize ourselves or someone else.

CaveWoman: She hijacks biology and seizes circuits, especially those involving motherhood. Smelling another's newborn can make a woman want her own child.[22] Once released from an ovary, a woman's egg will die or dissolve within twelve to twenty-four hours if fertilization doesn't occur, which creates a natural urgency for sex.

CaveMan: His basic, unchecked instinct is simple: spread the seed.

The Biological Clock

CaveWoman: In younger years, a flood of hormones can point a fertile woman toward a sizzle-male who can help her produce a healthy baby. Their chemistry may get them hot and bothered enough to marry and have children because "it's time," even if they don't possess the skills needed to maintain a lasting relationship.

CaveMan: Though males can produce offspring later in life, as age increases, it takes him longer to get a female pregnant. It takes up to five times longer for a man over forty-five years old to get a woman pregnant than if he was under twenty-five. His biological clock urges him to have plenty of sex earlier rather than later.[23]

On Mating Dances: Causing Sexual Attraction

The purpose of a mating dance is to cause sexual attraction. Because? Of course—babies!

CaveWoman: She's an expert at causing sexual attraction visually. A classic example is the appearance of a female dressed to the nines who stops traffic, or a scene where the sight of a woman causes suitors to swoon and fall at her feet. In my college days, hot pants (very short shorts) and boots were a thing. One day I wore dark green leather hot pants, tall boots, and a clingy sweater to a crowded lunchroom filled with young men from the upper eight floors of my dorm. I'll never forget what it was like to carry my food tray through this sea of men, how table conversations hushed suddenly and forks stopped in mid-air as I walked by. It was a powerful ego boost to cause sexual attraction and silence a group of hungry men.

CaveMan: Think exotic bird courtship here. The bowerbird builds a structure and decorates it with sticks and brightly colored objects in order to attract a mate. Other male birds dance a choreographed routine to entice nearby females. Some show off their vocal prowess or they spread their feathers while balancing on the remnants of a dead tree—a little bit like a male pole dance. Similarly, Caveman's approach is "here's what I know, what I own, and what I can do. If you like it, c'mon in. Be with me." He broadcasts his strongest features to attract a mate.

On Mating Dances: Reacting to Sexual Attraction

The cautionary tale for both men and women is that being under the steamy spell of a potential sexual partner can make us gush words that aren't true, smile yes when we mean no, dress to attract, purr even when wounded, or overspend energy, time, and resources in pursuit of the possibility of hot sex and a more exciting future.

CaveWoman: Notice the desire to please the male in a powerful position (the one who can mobilize your career), but don't fall for the invitation to his hotel room. Pay attention to CaveWoman's clothing advice for an encounter with someone to whom you're sexually attracted, then consciously decide what you wish to communicate through your selection of attire.

CaveMan: Recognize the natural, built-in frequency of your sexual urges, but make a choice to do what's appropriate, not what hormones dictate. Choose sex consciously, rather than as a default, or a right. This improves your ability to give (love and respect) rather than get (sex, instant gratification, something to conquer or boast about). Notice when you're feverishly attracted to a woman. Back away. When chemistry dominates, you will not treat a woman with the consideration and care she deserves.

Dealing with the Male Mating Dance

The notes in this section are double-edged. Women, get ready for head-on learning. Men, listen up. I'm speaking to women here about you when your CaveMan runs a conversation. The point here is to recognize when your CaveMan is active so you can ask him to step aside—be your awake and aware self instead. For both men and women, it is a kindness to view mating dances with compassion and wisdom. Here we go.

Women, if you find certain invitations to be curiously unromantic, remember that his request for your presence means he's attracted to you. He's hoping his speech will cast him in a favorable light and sway you to choose him. He's ruffling his feathers, offering you colorful reasons to stay around.

However, as you know by now, the behavior of our ancient selves isn't our wisest or most graceful foot forward. Give your connection with him a chance, even when CaveMan shows up first. If he focuses the conversation on himself, thank him for what he shares. What looks to you as self-centered is exactly that. And why? There's a double whammy at work here. Not only is this a cock-a-doodle-doo mating dance, but his approach to you is masculine, which begins with him at the center. Keep the faith. There's hope. We'll get there.

When a man talks about himself rather than engage the woman he invited on a date, this is CaveMan. By going on about himself, he aims to impress, which is, after all, the whole point of a mating dance. To influence your positive view of him, he'll invite you to situations where people know and respect him. If he's a self-assured speaker, he'll encourage you to attend his presentation. If he's prominent in business, your presence at a company event would be among his choices. As an experienced traveler, an invitation to join him on an excursion would show you the ease and luxury he enjoys and has to offer. If he's a confident lover, he'll look forward to sex with you as soon as possible.

The trouble women can encounter, especially on a first date, is that we listen more than we'd prefer. We feel bored or talked at, and head home dissatisfied. If we didn't alter the trajectory of the conversation, we're doubly upset, because we spent too much valuable time with "yet another male who didn't bother to get to know me."

The solution involves diplomacy between three of your aspects—CaveWoman, your masculine side, and true-you. Instead of being a polite pleaser, as CaveWoman would require, shift gears. Let the strength and focus of your masculine side kick in. Take the reins. First let your date know the reasons you went out with him. Be honest, be kind, be direct. Then invite him to get to know you. "Thank you for telling me about yourself. What would you like to know about me?" This request for a two-way conversation catapults you out of compliant CaveWoman and also invites him to step out of any surplus feather-ruffling.

Your positive action can result in relief for both of you. Even if you have no intention of accepting a second date, use the time with him as practice. Be straightforward, rather than dismissive or short-fused. Do what is necessary to take good care of yourself as you invite him out of CaveMan into a real conversation.

The Ways of CaveWoman

Here's another conversation with a double edge. It's about CaveWoman and is intended to educate both men and women. These examples of CaveWoman shed light on who she is and the types of messages she conveys. Notice which ones you recognize. These can serve as great discussion prompts for couples.

1. You promised your partner you'd make an important phone call but forgot. The clutch in your heart seems oddly disproportionate to this oversight. After all, the remedy is simple: pick up the phone and do what you forgot to do. The tension you feel isn't logical, yet it persists.

   CaveWoman's Translation: "I'm in danger. If my mate disapproves of me, I'll be thrown out of the cave, and I won't survive."

   Discussion: This example shows how our Survival Self influences us in relatively insignificant moments. Yes, the reaction is drastic. It's unrealistic—an illustration of how our Survival Self overestimates a threat. The tension produced is minor and short-lived. We override it and move on.

   To recognize our Survival Self favors the ability to lean toward our heart and soul, rather than our primal, reactive aspects. We can simply say, "I feel you, CaveWoman. Now let me make that forgotten phone call." Over time, this awareness makes a substantial difference in our ability to be expressive, confident, and free.

2. You feel compelled to correct a false rumor to save your reputation.

   CaveWoman's Translation: "Oh no! If my tribe believes this lie about me, I'll be rejected and be cast out. If the lions (critics) get me, that'll be the end."

Discussion: Whether or not it's important to correct a rumor is not the point here. What's key is how we feel compelled to adjust how others see us. For the most part, being misunderstood can be uncomfortable, but things tend to work out. Being worried about what others think of us is another example of threat miscalculation.

3. You feel pressure to agree with other women, especially in public. Today, during appetizers at lunch with your girlfriends, one of them describes "how stupid her husband was this week." The incident generates head-nodding and sympathy from the other women. When main dishes arrive, the second friend launches into an unflattering story about her male boss. Then a third describes trouble with her freedom-seeking seventeen-year-old son. Dessert brings your moment in the spotlight. You had considered sharing a turnaround experience regarding your husband's generosity, but you hesitate. The sisters at the table seem presently united against men, and to introduce a positive take on males feels stressful.

CaveWoman's Translation: "If I disagree with my sisters, then who will be on my side? I'll be left out."

Discussion: Logically speaking, this concern makes no sense, but your body pleads otherwise. Your heart rate is up, and you're a little short of breath—you're having a fight-or-flight experience. In the face of this tension, you opt to share a different story. CaveWoman prevails. It's okay. This is how awareness begins.

4. You are receiving a routine employee evaluation. As your supervisor begins to share details of your performance review, your stress level surges. You're tense, and shallow breathing ensues. You perspire as if actual danger is present.

CaveWoman's Translation: "Oh no! If I'm not perfect, I'll lose my job and have no money. I'll be despised, thrown out of the cave, and I'll die."

Discussion: CaveWoman comes from scarcity. Dig far enough, and you'll find she's always worried about death. CaveWoman reasons that if you ignore the carrot dangling in front of you (something positive), it's no big deal. There will be another carrot available soon. But if you ignore the boulder about to fall on your head (negative feedback about your job performance) or the tiger heading your way (any form of criticism), you could die, and that would be the end of you.

5. Your rough-and-tumble son is an adventurer. He's a climber, and you regularly discover him in high places. He's also curious and destroys toys to decipher how they're made. This morning you catch him as his paper clip heads for an electrical socket.

   CaveWoman's Translation: "What if I hadn't been here? What if he'd electrocuted himself?"

   Discussion: Even though you prefer not to panic, your voice gets loud. Any woman caring for a child (hers or someone else's) knows the tension produced during a protect-the-species moment. A few minutes later, even though the incident is over and the child is safe, it takes time to think calmly again.

   This is one of the harshest aspects of CaveWoman. Survival instincts cause us to be guilt-ridden about "could have, should have, would have." If the end result is failure (if the child dies) and instinct is calling the shots, there is no such thing as self-forgiveness. We kick ourselves out of the cave.

6. Someone asks a favor and you feel obligated but not inspired to say yes.

   CaveWoman's Translation: "I should help. If I'm a useful member of my tribe, I'll have food and shelter."

Discussion: Our Survival Self taps us to say yes when we'd prefer to say no. Awareness of this liberates us to consciously choose how to spend our time and energy.

~~~~~

Evolving Our Survival Selves

If we don't distinguish our Survival Self, we think that self is the whole of us. We think it's who we are. However, Survival Selves are part of us, not most or all of us. Especially, they are not the now you, the safe you, the happy you.

Survival Selves speak in specific and personal ways. Education, social or economic status, or upbringing do not extinguish the trumpet call of DNA. When you learn to recognize your CavePerson, be like a good neighbor and give a welcome nod. Then note whether your life is in danger or if it's a false alarm. If it's a false alarm, pat your CavePerson on the head and direct them to a seat. When you develop this kind of relationship with your CaveMama or CaveGuy, you're onto something life-changing.

1. To evolve your CavePerson, start small. At first, don't fix anything. Simply notice when your Survival Self is active in you as in, "Oh, there it is." This is important. I did that for months.

2. Once you're aware of the frequent visits from your Survival Self, choose actions you can execute even when you're tense, compelled, or sexually attracted. Note the advice from your CavePerson, but don't follow it. This might be harder than you think. It takes practice to come up with another way to be.

3. When you've got the first two steps down, combine them. Notice your CavePerson, take a breath, and go straight to true-you. Through practice, you can develop the awareness and skill to lead your Survival Self down from any cliff, in favor of the pleasure of expressing true-you.

PARTNERSHIP as EQUALS

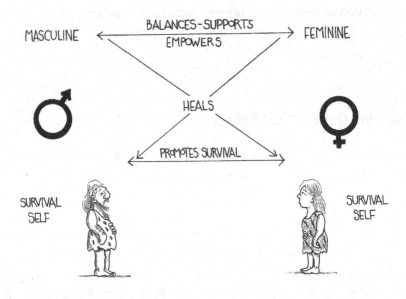

Illustration by David Cohen.

More Notes for Males

As with CaveWoman, to evolve CaveMan centers around noticing and managing reactions. Move out of CaveMan by summoning your feminine side (yes, you have "woman" in you). This requires that you recognize and value your feminine aspect. Remember the recommendation that women can take advantage of their masculine side instead of being a polite pleaser, as CaveWoman would require? For you, here's the flip side: you evolve your CaveMan when you welcome the versatile strength and expanded perspective of your feminine side. For example, the sudden snap to solve a problem through obliteration is your CaveGuy. When he urges you to pick up a verbal club to settle things, notice it but don't follow the advice. Rather than separate yourself from someone whose beliefs or actions you don't agree with or comprehend, as CaveMan would have you do, pull in your feminine abilities. Communicate. Listen. Build a bridge. Maybe there's more to the story, and to develop compassion or understanding would usher you toward a more balanced and resilient version of yourself, toward true-you.

Recognize your fierceness around the protection of others, but check whether your desire to protect prevents loved ones from making their own necessary choices. (Example: the story about Eric's interference with my closet customer.)

Recognize CaveMan's urge to veto through the use force or dominance. Notice when you resort to "Damn the torpedoes! Full speed ahead." Instead of declaring war or shouldering a gun, ask your inner diplomat to guide with balance and wisdom. Ask others to do this as well. That we can do better is in your hands.

Don't turn a blind eye. Make certain every woman on your payroll is paid equal to men. After you fix your situation, support others to do what's right. CaveMan comes from scarcity (not enough to go around, not enough for equal pay). Your masculine side can compartmentalize, and ignore injustice, inequality, and the suffering of others. Your feminine side cannot. Open to her. Pay attention to her. Listen to her. Recognize the dark side of the masculine, and call a halt to expression of it, for instance in exclusionary groups and "old boys clubs" where prejudice and privilege reign. Protect and support all people, not a chosen few.

Honor the Earth. Protect her. Nix the manufacture of products that harm the environment no matter how profitable they are or how they might benefit your family financially. Figure out an Earth-friendly solution. Say no to the code of greed. Think long-term health and well-being for all.

Find your sacred masculine—your feminine and masculine combined—and become it.

If We Knew More—Earlier

If knowing that we react to nonsurvival circumstances in survival-based ways was required knowledge for high school graduates, it would create reassurance during an otherwise confusing time. To be aware of how fight or flight impacts our intimate encounters would offer clarity to young men and women making hormone-fueled decisions in college.

For a newly married couple, information about our survival instincts would encourage connection and discussion.

With more awareness, we'd grasp that a harmonious relationship isn't necessary for survival. Knowing that we're not wired to get along, couples could forgive themselves. They would comprehend that being in love doesn't eliminate the challenge of living under the same roof. They'd realize that nothing is wrong with them, and that harmony is a learned bonus.

With a proper education about our Survival Selves, we'd navigate our early years with less flailing, confusion, and fear—or years of follow-up therapy. We'd make better decisions. We'd be easier on ourselves and more confident. Knowledge of our ancient, built-in aspects promotes patience with each other. All of us have work to do, and we can do it if we're committed to being aware and leading with the heart.

To understand our instinctual reactions is a valuable piece in the relationship puzzle, a giant step toward truth in self-expression and toward accord. But it is not the end of the story. Have compassion for your CavePerson, but let the soul of you—true-you—step up. This is a confidence-building, joyful experience that contributes to your ability to love yourself and your mate! Evolve your CavePerson. Find freedom.

~~~~~

Love is the bridge between you and everything.
—Rumi

13

Conversation: Is He Doing
What You Think He's Doing? Part 1

I HOPE YOU enjoyed the main course. Next, a well-earned dessert: a conversation with a client that brings all of this to a sweeter place. She discovers that her interpretations of her husband's words and actions are inaccurate, which surprises her. It is also emotional. One way to read this interaction is to hear her questions as your questions and soak up her shifts. An advantage of immersing ourselves in another's story is that we learn along with them. Welcome to her excellent work.

This client has a proactive learning style. After adding to her cache of understanding, she reaches for more. Her willingness to remain open allows new questions to bubble up, and she explores them. Initial sessions with me were solo (without her husband), which granted her the opportunity to express in the freest way possible. She speaks her mind, tries things. She falls over and gets back up. She's a spunky one!

~~~~~

Note: Commentary about the session, intended to guide and inform you, is in italics and indented, like this.

ME: You've mentioned several issues. If you could have relief about one principle matter, what would it be?

HER: I'm ready to dive into the subject of communication between me and my husband. It seems basic and important.

ME: You mentioned that both of you have developed hearing issues. What do you not want to hear from him?

HER: Here's an example. I say, "Do you see that branch out there hanging on the tree? I think it's going to fall down, and it might hit something." He says, "No, it's pretty well hooked up there. It's not going to fall down." When he's being oppositional, I'd rather turn my hearing aids off. There's no flow in the conversation. He's a conversation stopper.

ME: It sounds like the two of you could use some help receiving each other. When you receive someone's communication, there's a natural back-and-forth, a give-and-take, right?

HER: Which is exactly what happens when I talk to my women friends. So why do I have so much trouble with my husband?

ME: Good question. Why might that be?

HER: I'm sure that's because, as you say, we don't receive each other. How do I change that with my husband?

ME: Start tiny. With unimportant subjects.

HER: Okay...

ME: To undo a communication pattern the two of you have practiced for a good while, start easy. Pay attention to your responses to him. For instance, did you welcome his communication, or did you have a snap reaction against it? Then acknowledge to yourself, for instance: "I see that I disagreed and pushed back." The point is that you notice a reaction, instead of being in the reaction. Step outside it, and observe it. Yes? Are we good so far?

HER: We're good.

How About a Little Improv?

ME: Have you ever seen a performance by an improvisation group? [She nods.] Then you know that what they do is based on agreement and ongoing expansion of the agreement. When a player says a chair is black, the rule is that you don't go against. You don't say to the audience, "Actually, he meant it's white." You agree and add. To resist the creative choice of another player causes the scene to fall apart fast. But when actors agree and add, the audience is on the edge of their seats.

HER: You know, that's actually what I want him to do when I say, "The branch is going to fall." He could say, "Yes, I see the branch. And I can see how you might be concerned, but you know, I've checked it, and it looks pretty well hooked up there. I don't think we need to worry about it." That's actually all I need!

ME: Have the two of you ever talked about this "yes, and..." idea?

HER: No. I'm too busy hating him for being oppositional! This one simple change would make such a difference. [Then her face and shoulders soften.] The other thing, which I never saw until this moment, is that he actually isn't oppositional all the time... How did I possibly miss that?

ME: Interesting, huh?

HER: He actually doesn't oppose me...most of the time! I get upset when he does, and then my mind decides that's how he communicates with me. But it's not accurate.

ME: Well, how great to see it! And it was easy for you, wasn't it? See what happens when you back up a few paces to observe what you're doing? [She nods.] May I run something else by you? Another aspect?

HER: Sure.

ME: Is it possible that your husband is trying to do a good thing when he tells you not to worry about the branch?

HER: How could that be? What do you mean?

ME: Is it possible that he wants to take care of your fear—send the big, bad fear wolf away from your door? Is it possible he's aiming to do a good thing?

HER [crying softly]: I see what you're saying. I don't allow him to help me feel safe. Not at all!

ME: He may not realize that you trust through agreement. If he said, "yes, and…" he'd be agreeing with you, which comforts you and opens trust, and then you'd be better able to hear his opinion about the branch, that it won't fall, and you can feel safe.

HER: Totally. I missed what he was trying to do for me. But the irony is that, in general, I feel unsafe with him. He's forgetful, loses everything.

> *Notice what she's doing here. She perceives what we've been talking about and now stretches for more on the subject.*

Where Does Safety Come From?

ME: How do you view safety, meaning who is responsible for your feeling of safety?

HER: I am. It boils down to me. I just don't know how to feel safe in the face of some of his actions. He makes me feel unsafe. Wait. No, he doesn't. I feel unsafe when he does certain things. I can do something about that, I'm sure. I just don't know how to feel calm and centered when he's losing things left and right.

ME: Good catch there, about being the generator of whether you feel safe or not. Thank you for that.

HER: I felt the shift as I was talking. It's exciting to self-correct. When my husband says the branch will not fall, it's possible he wishes to make my world safer. What a mind-blowing idea to consider his intention.

ME: Yes. This would indicate he's for you, not against you. He may not even be conscious of making an effort to protect you or make you feel safe. It comes naturally. But, in truth, nobody else can make you *feel* safe except you.

It's similar to how we are beautiful yet hold ourselves as unattractive. We can be talented and at the same time convinced we're not. We can be handed a golden opportunity while thinking of ourselves as undeserving. Can others convince us of our beauty, talent, or worth? No. It's an inside job. The safety issue is like that. It's an inside job. By the way, do you think he's tried to make you feel safe before, and now you realize it?

HER: I'm sure I thought it was something else entirely, like he's ignoring what I want, or trying to control me or dismiss me—who knows what I thought—but I'm sure I didn't give the benefit of the doubt.

ME: There are so many ways men look out for us, and we miss it. We miss it now, perhaps because of the traceable history of men in control of women. Terrible injustices have occurred in the past and continue today. But at this exact moment with your husband, what's true? That's the only fair question. Could you give him the benefit of the doubt, such as he loves me and is p-r-o-b-a-b-l-y trying to say or do something good. What is it?

HER: So… interesting…!!!

Now witness a remarkable event! Something in the way she understands her husband shifted, and her brain begins to reorganize the meaning and significance of past events. I've seen this previously on the faces and in the bodies of clients when a lifetime of old data begins to re-sort itself.

What had been categorized as a negative experience is being recategorized because what she thought happened didn't. Connections in her brain are changing to match the new interpretation. This illustrates Marie Monfils's research, that new information transforms an old memory. Once the process starts, it continues over hours, days, and weeks. A year later, when my client looks back, she'll be astonished at how much she has changed.

ME: You are shifting fast right now. Can you feel it?

HER: Yes. I'm not sure who I am now. I don't know quite what to do! Or how to be! Or what really went on in my past!

ME: I remember that feeling so well!

She learned something new (he's possibly doing a good thing; he intends to help me feel safe), and it sent shock waves through her. This transformation (it's radical, not step-by-step) generates an abrupt disconnect from her usual thought patterns. In order to accommodate this event, her brain severs thousands of old neural connections.

Think of the moment in the early days of telephones, when switchboard operators connected callers by inserting a pair of phone plugs into the appropriate jacks. This moment with my client compares to operators across a continent unplugging thousands of connected conversations simultaneously and then sitting back in their chairs. In the field of neuroplasticity this is known as unlearning. For more on this, check out the work of Norman Doige, especially The Brain that Changes Itself.

We take a significant pause while she sighs, makes funny sounds, laughs, and cries a little. When things slow down, I check in with her.

ME: Are you ready for interaction? Or shall we wait?

HER: It's okay. Thank you for the pause. I needed that. Now I can let my brain do what it's doing and still hear you.

Do It for You

ME: I want to talk with you about something vital to your process. [She nods.] Don't make changes for him. Make changes for you. Don't do something only for him. The reason you do anything is first and foremost for you.

HER: Make changes for me. Not him?

ME: Yes. He'll benefit from your developments, but that's not why you initiate them. Your goal isn't to please someone else, or to conform. Don't make changes because you feel you owe him. Or because you think you should. Or to be a good wife. Or to keep the peace. Make changes for one reason: to be the person you came here to be.

HER: I get it. Thanks. I absolutely needed that.

At this point in our conversation, my job is to find highly reactive places in her growing sense of things. We'll find some emotional land mines together, instead of leaving them to happen at home. To accomplish this, I'll do a review and circle back through points covered earlier. One point is the idea of receiving him.

ME: Let's review your focus in the coming days. Listen to him, be open to him. Breathe in what he says and does. Receive him.

HER: Okay.

ME: At the beginning of our time today, we talked about how to be the watcher of the woman having a reaction, that when he says or does something that upsets you, take a deep breath and pause. Notice your reaction. Notice you didn't receive him.

HER: Okay. I'm sure that's going to happen. A big ugly wind will come, and I'll fly backward against a wall. All right, I notice my reaction. Then what?

ME: Name your reaction. "I'm angry." Then say why you think you're upset. "Because he's being oppositional." As soon as you can, remember to be curious instead of accusatory. Put your brain to work on "What if he's for me, not against me?" Or "What if he's doing something good? What is it?"

> *I'm about to ask her for an ordinary trouble spot, so we can reinforce the mind-bending idea "he's for me, not against me."*

ME: Can you provide a hot-off-the-press example of what he might do or say that irritates you and causes you to react?

Working with a Trouble Spot

HER: This morning, I was irritated about the kitchen and said to him, "Could you please not get honey all over the countertop and cupboard handle when you have honey on your morning toast? I don't like to get it all over my fingers."

ME: Excellent, thank you. What kind of communication was that?

HER: Negative. My voice was not nice at all.

ME: Was it criticism?

HER: Oh, most certainly.

ME: You gave him a complaint, right?

HER: Yes. I have lots of those! Well, what am I supposed to do? Clean up the DAMN HONEY and plaster a smile on my face?

Okay! There's a land mine. Good for us. We found one. Land mines often show up when we apply a new idea.

ME [gently]: No, don't clean up the damn honey and plaster a smile on your face...no, not so much! Don't put up with or pretend. If you do, you'll collect—oh, five or ten or twenty resentments—and then explode! That's when things get really mean and messy.

She realizes how strongly she reacted and begins to rock back and forth on her chair to let all that energy loose. She's doing her assignment. She's noticing her reaction.

ME: Good job! You noticed! [She gives two thumbs up.] What if you query him? "Do you know you leave honey smears on the counter and on the handle of the cupboard after you spread honey on your morning toast?" He will then tell you. Until you ask him, you don't really know.

HER: Nope, I don't. That may end the whole thing. He might say, "I had no idea I was leaving honey tracks. I'm sorry. That won't happen again."

ME: Exactly. And then it's over with! In other situations, you might say, "I have a request. Do you have time to talk about it? It would take five or ten minutes." If there's not enough time, make an appointment with each other.

HER: So, let me say it... "I have a request. Do you have five or ten minutes to talk?" Okay, I can do that. That's good.

ME: There's a second part. Say a phrase such as:

"By the way, I'm not upset with you..."

"You're not in trouble with me..."
"You're not in the doghouse. I just want to talk about something I need."

HER: Well, he IS in trouble with me! I can't LIE about it!

ME: True. He is. Your work before you discuss anything is to release him from trouble.

HER: How could I possibly do that? Why should I do that? Wait—what exactly is my work?

ME: To accept what he did.

> Carl Jung said, "We cannot change anything until we accept it."
>
> An angry request creates a pressure-filled demand. It's almost impossible for someone to give (freely) what you command, because they don't have a choice.
>
> For a while here, we do nothing but breathe and sit. What a perfect pause for some good science. Research by HeartMath Institute tells us that how we respond to a stimulus determines the neural pathways activated in our brain and between our brain and our heart.
>
> "If you respond with any form of initial negativity (which translates physiologically as constriction)—freezing, bracing, clinging, clenching, and so on—the pathway illumined leads to your amygdala (or "reptilian brain," as it's familiarly known)... which controls a repertory of highly energized fight-or-flight responses. If you can relax into a stimulus—opening, softening, yielding, releasing—the neural pathway leads through the more evolutionarily advanced parts of your forebrain and, surprisingly, brings brain and heart rhythms into entrainment."[24]

This is why it's important to accept what he did (get to neutral) before attempting a conversation. Wisdom is available when our heart and brain rhythms are in sync.

ME: To accept what he did doesn't constitute approval or agreement, by the way. I'm saying that your work is to first make his honey tracks less of a big deal in your mind. Can you do that?

HER: I could, but I don't want to.

Her confession surprises me and sends us both into laughter! How splendid to be able to express her sense of humor in the middle of an upset!

What if Nobody's in the Doghouse?

ME: Letting him off the hook would be too hard?

HER [gasps, still laughing]: Yes, actually.

ME [smiling]: Why?

HER: Then I'd be wrong instead of him. He should be wrong.

ME: But what if nobody's wrong?

HER: What?!?

ME: What if nobody's wrong?

HER: Nobody's wrong? I don't think that way, do I?

ME: Many of us decide pretty regularly who's right and who's wrong.

HER: I decide who and what is right all day long. I'm picky.

ME: To have preferences is different from concluding that something is wrong. Preferences are fun and fabulous if you don't get too attached to them. The conclusion that your husband is wrong because he is different from you is what we're talking about here. Do you see the distinction?

HER: Now I do. You're right. I would need to state "you're not in the doghouse" prior to a conversation with my husband and mean it, because, well, you see, he gets in trouble with me quite regularly—unfortunately! If I asked for time to talk, he'd be certain he's in trouble with me.

But putting him in the doghouse isn't what I want to do. That doesn't make me happy. What woman wants *that*? It's no fun to dislike the person you live with. Besides, criticizing him doesn't change him. Why doesn't criticism work?

ME: Does criticism work on you?

HER: What do you mean?

ME: Does criticism affect you? Do you change, even a little, when someone criticizes you?

HER: I see your point. Yes, criticism affects me. I think about what was said and then avoid that person. Or I get tense in the presence of that person. Or I try not to offend them again in the future. That sort of thing.

ME: We do to others what we do to ourselves. If criticism works on us, we pass it on.

HER: That's true, isn't it? Criticism works on me, so I use it on him.

~~~~

This completes part one of this conversation. The second half continues in the next chapter.

~~~~~

We are all alchemists transmuting pain into aliveness,
unwanted experiences into awakening.
—Rashani Rea

14

Conversation: Is He Doing
What You Think He's Doing? Part 2

IT'S NATURAL TO make progress in fits and starts. You'll see this client continue to move through strong emotions, even to blow sky-high, as she heads toward better communication with her husband. She gets angry, feels sorry for herself, and is powerfully centered, all in the space of a session.

Our conversation continues.

~~~~~

HER: You mean I might be a yo-yo for a while?

ME: You might. Any steep learning curve includes mistakes, falls, and confusion—two steps forward, one step back.

HER: Okay, I get it.

ME: When you've made time to talk with him and you're ready to ask for what you need, say something nice to him first.

HER: Oh, gawd, really? Why do I need to do that? I don't want to bother with that. Why should I do that? No!!!

I was pretty sure my suggestion would cause her to fume. It's one of her buttons. You saw it already with the honey-on-the-counter example. ("Shall I just plaster a smile on my face and clean up the damn honey?") This request to say something nice to him obliges her to get to a state of acceptance before initiating a conversation. We're still working on that.

ME: This step is important. Don't even bother to talk with him unless you can say something affirmative. This is an excellent way to check whether you're in shape to have a conversation. It's proof he's not in the doghouse.

She looks at me like I'm nuts. She's all undone.

HER: No! I don't want to do that! I refuse!

ME [with huge love]: This is the yo-yo thing. Moments ago you worked your way through the honey tracks scenario, and now you're sideways about being nice to him.

We wait in silence. She'll relax about this, but she needs time to spit and sputter. This is what progress looks like. This is what it takes for the brain to unlearn an old habit and consider a new option. Old connections must unplug themselves. For sure, she's unplugging!

HER [slowly nodding and looking down at her lap]: Yeah…

Before moving on, we cover more about having compassion for herself for blowing sky-high. We also talk about how effective it is to request something from another person rather than demand it. When there's no demand, the person can give what you're asking for as a gift. Now back to the idea of "be nice to him."

ME: How might you say something nice to him?

HER: OH GAWD. I just don't think he deserves my niceness.

She nearly falls off the chair to demonstrate her reluctance. I'm so appreciative of her ability to be present to her strong emotions and attitudes, and to act them out!

ME: Do you deserve kindness?

HER: Of course.

ME: Is he different from you?

HER: What?

ME: Maybe your husband deserves kindness, too?

HER: Oh, all right…he does. Sure, he does. Crap.

ME: You can only offer him what you have. You can give your husband "kind you" if you've been practicing kind you *with you.*

HER: Sorry, can't find "kind me" right now.

ME: She's gone under the covers, hasn't she? It's all right. She'll come back out when she's ready. [I reach over and touch her arm.] Again, this is the yo-yo effect. You take two steps forward because you've had an epiphany, and with the suggestion to be kind to him prior to an important conversation you fly backward into the wall. This is the ugly wind you mentioned a while back.

To relax the pace here and give her a bit of a break, I'll retrace some steps and repeat information. We'll see how it sits with her this time around.

ME: Do you know why being able to say something kind to him prior to a conversation matters?

HER: Nope. Not in a million friggin' years.

ME: It's a litmus test.

> *After a few seconds, she motions for me to go on, even though her body language tells me she's still feeling sarcastic. I proceed with caution.*

ME: If you can say something kind to him, you're in shape for a conversation. If you can't say something kind, you're not ready. Talk another time.

HER [taking a long, slow sigh]**:** Makes sense. Totally.

> *With this, she gets off her chair and lies down on the floor. She's flat on her back, looking up at the ceiling. This astonishes me. I'm now speaking to a woman on the floor. Nobody's ever done that in thirty-five years of private sessions.*

HER: I just gotta change positions. It helps. Okay. What's the question?

ME: How can you say something kind to him?

HER: I mean…does it have to be something…? I mean…well…could it be something like "Thank you for going to the grocery store"?

ME: It can be exactly that. An expression of gratitude can be really, really simple.

- I noticed you straightened up the laundry room—thanks!
- Thanks for hauling away the piles of brush after I trimmed the bushes.
- Thanks for volunteering to cook dinner last night; that made such a difference in my evening.

Do you know another reason to get to neutral before talking to him?

HER: No. But I can't wait to hear it.

ME [smiling about her retort]: It's a measure of whether your heart is open. If your heart is open, your ears can hear. You won't be "hard of hearing."

HER: Oh. We're back to hard of hearing. Ugh. Then for sure my heart could use a little opening.

ME: You can check whether you have an open heart by offering a thank-you, by giving a compliment and meaning it. Then talk to him about your honey concern:

> "I noticed I got frustrated in the kitchen this morning when I tried to make my breakfast. There was honey on the counter, the toaster, the handle of the fridge. I love when the kitchen is clean, and I can make my breakfast easily. When I come home—if it's still clean—I can do whatever I want to do in the kitchen. A clean space makes me really happy."

HER: I get it. I don't do that, but now I can do that.

She gets up off the floor and back into her chair.

ME: See how your communication stirs him. Maybe it prompts a discussion. Then maybe continue with, "When you leave honey all over the place and it gets on the outfit I'm wearing, all over my fingers, I start swearing. It's w-a-y harder to like anyone when I'm swearing. If the honey thing gets fixed, then hey, no problem!"

HER: Honestly, that would make my husband laugh out loud. I'd never see honey tracks again. [She waves her hands in the air with a big sweep.] Problem solved!

ME: Yes, problem solved because you're coming from love and delight, knowing this honey thing is no big deal.

Her List

HER [spontaneously consults her notes and reads a list of what we've talked about]: Let me see if I've got this.

- Notice conclusions I've come to, for instance, thinking he's oppositional all the time...Is it actually true?
- Practice receiving him. Use the improvisation idea "yes and..." Pay attention to when I receive him and when I don't.
- Assume he's for me, not against me. He's probably doing something good. Look for what it might be.
- I'm in charge of *feeling* safe.
- Steps to a conversation: Check to see if I'm neutral. Say something nice to him. [She laughs about this now.] Tell him I want to talk, ask if he has time. Tell him he's not in the doghouse and make sure it's true.
- Instead of criticizing honey tracks in the kitchen, focus on what I love, like I love a clean kitchen.

What a good list. I'll give you an example of how I could have done something differently had I known what I do now. Okay?

> *Again, she volunteers to put new information to work. How brilliant. How proactive!*

ME: Go for it.

HER: Here's what happened. My husband walked into the kitchen and said, "You won't believe this, but a magazine just bought my story, and they are asking me to resend it because they can't find the copy I sent them." I said, "Wow, that's crazy!" Then he said, "And what's *really* crazy is that I can't find *my* copy of the story either!" How can this man be so x!@#★ disorganized? It was horrible what was going on in my head.

ME: What could you have done differently?

HER: I could have said, "Wow, that's crazy. I can't imagine how they lost your story." [She stops and thinks.] Should I tell him I'll help him find it?

ME: That's stepping in to solve his problem. He didn't ask for that.

HER: Okay, that's good, because I don't really want to help him find his story. I could say, "I'm sure you'll find it. Let me know if I can help you in some way."

ME: Yes, better. But start with a positive, your acknowledgment of his win. This is the say-something-nice-to-him part. Point the focus of the conversation to the winning aspect of what took place. "I'm thrilled for you that they're publishing your story! Congratulations! I'm sure you'll find it. Let me know if I can help you in some way."

HER: Okay. That sounds good.

Another Wave of Pissed Off

HER [with a mocking tone]: I have great faith that you will find the manuscript—you who can't find anything or get organized! [She looks me directly in the eyes.] It feels like you're putting the whole thing on me.

> *She's suddenly yelling. Do you find this outburst to be an odd turn of events? If clients feel free enough, this is one way they work out the leftovers after a shift in consciousness. They act out the reactions and attitudes that plague them most often. It's a good thing.*
>
> *This is probably what happens at home when nobody's looking. It's another land mine. She's taking advantage of how the two of us—together—can investigate what she does. We're partners in this. Things are about to get more intense before they smooth out. I'll play into her resistance here and help her dump it.*

ME: You're right. It's all on you. This is in your lap.

HER: Why?

ME: He's not here. He's not asking. You're asking.

HER: Will you talk to him like this?

ME: I will. But his lap is different from yours. His orientation to these circumstances includes other factors and variances. Here's the tricky part, and I know this from personal experience. The point you're raising highlights why it took me so many years to create a happy marriage. Ready?

HER: Maybe.

ME: Please tell me more about "maybe..."

HER: Well, it's that things have to be partly his fault.

ME: We've talked about how you can't solve a problem if you've decided it's his fault. Then you're dependent on him for things to change.

HER: Dammit.

ME: Do you want to change the pattern of making things his fault?

HER: What if I say yes to that?

ME: Then you have to do something different, instead of asking him to be different.

HER: I can't say I'm wild about that.

ME: If your happiness depends on someone else acting a particular way, you have no power at all.

HER: Wait, say WHAT???

I take a moment to breathe consciously and slow things down here, to help her breathe and slow down, too.

ME: If your happiness depends on specific actions from others, then you are a leaf in the wind, and you blow wherever that big, ugly wind takes you.

HER: Okay. I have to tell you how much I hate this. But—the way I'm doing things isn't working. At all.

ME: Wouldn't it be delightful to feel fulfilled and happy?

HER: Yes.

ME: Wouldn't it be lovely to spend your later years in bliss and joy?

HER: Oh, wait! Let's not get carried away here! Getting rid of my inner angry bitch would be a really good thing, though.

ME: Then let's see what we can do about that.

Don't Do to Others What Never Worked for You

HER: I'm not sure where you're going with this. My angry bitch is blocking my hears—I mean my ears.

Next I illustrate my talking points with elaborate sound effects and gestures. I've got wrenches in my hands, grenades to throw, and long arms. You'll see what I mean.

ME: To fix others in order for us to be happy involves the constant reach into their world to mess with them. We move into their brains to rearrange their thoughts. We position little bombs in there to blow up what we consider to be unacceptable ways of thinking. We try to teach them how to act and what to believe. We are demanding, controlling, nitpicky. It's exhausting.

> *She laughs out loud. We have a jovial moment about my air art and special sound effects. Her past history is key here. She gets this. This is big. Then I lean forward for emphasis.*

ME: The use of hammers, wrenches, and screwdrivers doesn't change other people. Around you, they downplay their opinions and withhold information. As soon as they depart, poof—they return to being authentic and real. Think about your father and all the tinkering he did with you. Did you like all the tinkering?

HER: No, I hated him—and the tinkering.

ME: So don't become him.

HER: Ugh!

ME: Don't do to your husband what your father did to you. Jung said, "Until you make the unconscious conscious, it will direct your life and you'll call it fate." [There's a long pause here. She's wide-eyed.] Or how about this from Richard Rohr: "Pain that is not transformed is transmitted."[25]

HER: Oh, wow. Look what I've done...

ME: You have a choice about whether to pass to others what never worked for you. You can call a halt to a family pattern. You can heal it by not repeating it.

HER: I'm up for it.

ME: So...you've got no power if...

HER: ...you attempt to control other people to be happy.

135

ME: And you do have the capacity to influence if ...

HER: ...everything is in my lap.

ME: When we're talking about power here, we're not talking about power over someone else of course. We're saying you have the ability to change your perspective, which alters what you experience and what you conclude. That's where healing lives. You can move from "he's against me, he's oppositional" to "how is he helping?" You can ask, "What's he doing that's good? How is he *for me*?" You can elect to treat your husband differently than how your father treated you.

HER: I've been doing things the hard way. No wonder I'm tired.

> *She pauses and looks down at her lap. Her eyes close, and her head tips to the right. Both of her hands come together in prayer position. She brings her prayer hands up and tucks them under her right ear as if she's going to sleep. She rests there for a long moment. Then her head rises slowly, her arms fall back to her lap, and she begins to speak.*

HER: I have to tell you something that really bothers me about all of this.

ME: I'm all ears.

HER: The thing that's so deeply embedded in me is that my husband gets to do whatever he wants, and I have to fix things. I resent that.

ME: Many people voice this precise frustration. That's how I felt, too.

HER: Really? Are you serious?

ME: I'm serious. I sincerely believed I was making adjustments, and Eric was slacking off. But, in truth, at the end of the day I was actually doing what I accused him of doing—of course I was! This is how it works. I've been married three times. Eric was number four. Plus, I had two other significant relationships, including one with the father of my daughter. I changed significant relationships every five years or so.

My client did not know this about me. Her jaw drops. She scoots forward in her chair in anticipation.

ME: A few years into knowing Eric, I arrived at the same exact standstill, the place where the relationship crashes, goes up in flames, turns to ashes. That's when the hallelujah light went on inside me. "Oh, it's not about whether my partner changes! It's about me doing my work. If I do my work, it changes me, and also changes us."

HER: Surprise, surprise! I had no idea! What did you do?

ME: I studied, took classes, researched like crazy, and experimented as if I knew nothing at all about partnership. I reevaluated my approach to men and marriage. I took responsibility for my happiness by making the changes we've talked about today.

HER: Wow. I'm so ready to do all of this! I'm in a beautiful new home that I love so much. This work I'm doing with you is a part of what's new. I'm saturated, full to the brim. Thank you.

ME: Yes, that's a wrap!

~~~~~

Acceptance is the universal currency of real friendship...
It does not warp or shape or wrench a person to
be anything other than what they are.
—Sister Joan Chittister

We are made of star stuff.

—Carl Sagan

PART THREE

Five Core Skills for Making Changes

15

Core Skill #1: Breathe

MY FRIEND GIUSEPPE would surely be Santa Claus if he weren't a massage therapist. When I showed up for an appointment and was clearly in a stressed state, he said with a twinkle, "How are you?" My answer: "I'm fine." And then the belly laughing began.

It's delightful to tell a bit of a lie, knowing that your friend realizes it. It's especially enjoyable if stretching the truth is invited, which to my way of thinking it was, twinkly eyes and all. On the massage table, Giuseppe asked me why I was sideways about life, and I blurted a few reasons. In response, he said this brilliant, simple thing. "Whatever seems troubling, you ought to just breathe about it." Then he rolled up his sleeves and kneaded the stress out of my body.

"Breathe about it" drops us out of worry and distress, because it's impossible to think a troubled thought while breathing with awareness. When I'm attentive to my breath, my senses open and my perspective expands to the beauty of the world around me. I had no part in the growth of the tall trees outside my door, yet there they are, and what a miracle! To watch a blue swallowtail butterfly float by my office window wasn't on my to-do list, but it showed up, wings and all. My talents do not include vehicle design, and still it is my daily pleasure to drive a car. The Earth rotates, the sun rises over the horizon, and the moon appears without reminders or prompts. When I breathe about it, I tune in to the miracles that surround me.

We are here because we are being breathed. We are being inspired. If Source is breathing us, then Source's wisdom comes in on our breath as well. In the stillness of the breath, attention is removed from surface appearances and personality, and we take in the peace that holds us.

That "Breathe About It" Feeling

In glorious September–October weather, I often did yoga on the cobblestone sidewalk outside my home. When a single leaf fell from the top of a sixty-foot tree to my shoulders while I was doing triangle pose or downward-facing dog, that felt intensely intimate. Some leaves floated. Others plummeted. Falling leaves relaxed me and gave me the "breathe about it" feeling.

Do you regularly engage in activities or experiences that encourage you to breathe slowly enough to enjoy the miracle of ordinary moments? Do you relax into the colors of the beads you string, the elasticity of the dough in your hands, the cool drops of rain on your face? Do you appreciate the strength of your legs as you hike? Did you luxuriate in the sweetness of holding your child just now? Whatever pleases you, make sure you have adequate doses in your day and week. With enough banked pleasure, during stress you're more likely to remember to breathe about it.

Life turns out okay eventually. Events unfold. Though they might not be what we expected or thought we wanted, focusing on the breath is a way to begin to accept something difficult. It took me a good, long while to find peace after the death of my husband. Breathing about it eventually led me to trust his departure. After all, who was I to second-guess the proper length of Eric's journey? Who was I to doubt his time to die?

Events in our lives are a benefit somehow, some way, even if they don't appear to be at first. Betrayal becomes a catalyst for restoring faith in ourselves. Loss leads to an eventual gain. The marriage that went sideways? There's a silver lining, though it might take time to show up.

We find our way to acceptance and appreciation sooner rather than later if we take a pause and let it be.

Breathing about it invites good things to float to us like leaves falling down. Conscious breathing stills us enough to remember all the ways that life is *for us*. Yesterday's drudgery, or those demanding years with two jobs and three children, or the romantic endeavor that never quite found its feet—each of these contributed mightily to you. If you learn from hardships, you look back and call them adventures.

Especially if you breathe about it.

~~~~~

You are where you need to be. Just take a deep breath.

—Lana Parrilla

16

Core Skill #2: Receive

OUR BREATH MAKES way for the second core skill: receive. This sounds basic, doesn't it? Someone offers information, we listen. Someone gives a gift, we thank them and unwrap it. However, to receive doesn't always involve taking in what's easy. It also means we find a way to accept words, thoughts, or actions that go against our beliefs. We invite our partner to bring their whole self to a conversation, to parenting, or to lovemaking, including the parts we find difficult.

To receive my husband means to know and accept what he does, how he thinks, what he believes—which is different from what I do, how I think, and what I believe. There is no push from me, no demand for him to be more of something or less of something. I see him. I pay attention to what inspires him and take note of what supports him, troubles him, matters to him. To receive him is to appreciate who he is *as he is*, because I've offered the same kindness and consideration to myself. Learning to accept myself has prepared me to welcome all of *him*, all of *us*, as we are.

Practice: Receive Easy Situations

Work your way toward receiving difficult situations by starting with easy ones. Begin with noticing your ability to give attention to an ordinary moment. When the act of receiving is a casual, daily practice, it prepares you to welcome tougher circumstances when they arise. This is similar to how meditation contributes to an easier, calmer day. Below are examples to imagine in an unhurried way. Appreciate the simplicity of these situations and how they invite your senses to inform you.

Stroll through a garden on a spring morning as the light comes up. Notice the burst of new life. What is blooming? Listen as you walk. Let your attention visit your feet. Sense the temperature of the air on your skin.

Stand at your kitchen sink as morning sun pours through the window near you. Notice the warm water as it runs through your fingers, the smell of lemon verbena soap, the freshness of a clean towel.

Feel your muscles as you power walk on your lunch break. Give attention to how your arms pull forward and back. The wind whips your hair as you round the street corner, and the surprise makes you laugh.

A leisurely evening stroll on the beach bathes you in the blazing peach and yellow colors of the Pacific Ocean sunset. Salt and seaweed infuse the air you breathe. The warmth of the day lingers in the sand beneath your bare feet. While taking in the final moments of the sun as it dips behind faraway waves, you enjoy a cool drink at your favorite open-air restaurant.

Walk out of your city apartment into city sounds and, for a moment, remain perfectly still. Marvel at the bustling vigor, the buoyant energy of activities around you, including the steady patience of those who walk without hurry.

It's early morning as you stroll into your local bakery and exchange smiles with the owner. Your eyes sweep the display of artwork on the walls, and the wafting aromas of coffee and sweet cinnamon cause a quick rise in your spirit. A chocolate croissant arrives on a stark white plate, and you tear it open. Your taste buds kick in—oh, the butter!

Are you all there? Awake and aware? What do you feel? Are your senses open, awash in what a single, simple moment offers? This is receiving at its easiest.

Practice: Receive Easy People

Now, how about stepping up your practice, this time to receive humans? Again, at first choose neutral or mildly pleasant situations.

As you clean up after dinner, your family spreads to various areas of your home. Children head to their rooms to finish homework. On the way, your son plays with the dog, and your daughters discuss an incident from school today. You observe activity, intention, speed of movement as your husband and his dinner guest retire to the deck for an ongoing visit. They are visible through large sliding glass doors, a view that extends out over a wide valley and to mountains beyond. Both men are animated, alternately telling stories and listening. There is a strong connection between them, and you catch the exuberance in their gestures and the vital energy of their laughter.

In a situation where you receive, offer your undivided attention. Do your best to note details without evaluation. At dinner tomorrow evening, be with your husband as if you've never before met him. How does he breathe, sit, use his fork? Where do his hands rest during a meal? How does he rise from a chair?

Practice this art of receiving humans for a good while. Take time to develop confidence and ease with it and also to appreciate the attention it necessitates. When you give yourself to the quiet in the presence of others, see what there is to receive, to learn.

What's Next?

When you've taken time to receive what's easy, move on to events, people, or situations that tend to be trickier, those charged with more emotion. If you notice you're not receiving, simply meet the resistance where it is—no need to make it vanish—though you might be able to soften it with a few deep breaths.

Here's an everyday example of becoming conscious of a reaction (not receiving), followed by an intentional shift to receive. My hunter cat, Bella, sometimes brought live animals into our house. We discovered that she adored having playthings, and they were not always mice. There were chipmunks, birds, and baby black snakes, too. Today there's a mouse in my house, and he's found his way into my office.

My receiving practice:

> At first I groan. My shoulders fall and my head tips forward. With a sigh, I realize I'm not receiving the mouse who scampers about, delivered by a cat I love.

> So, I breathe about it and ask, "What's true?" There's a critter in my work space, making its way around the room behind furniture. Will it hurry across my foot or run up my leg while I'm typing? Or will it leave me alone?

> Thankfully, I'm able to concentrate. As I am on a writing break thirty minutes later, Mr. Mouse scoots out of my office door and down the hall. Eric helps me block the little guy's path with a couple of long boards. We open the front door, and the mouse runs outside. That was easy!

An average day gives us plenty of practice with acceptance (receiving). A traffic pileup prevents us from getting to an appointment, causes a reschedule, and a dose of temporary angst. How did we do with receiving that? Or how about when your daughter approaches, upset. Can you hear her words and sense her emotion but not join her trouble? Do your best to avoid commentary or advice and ask open questions such as, "Is there anything else you'd like me to know?" to solicit more from her. See if you can welcome her communication without an attempt to improve the situation. Simply receive what's there, and offer the grace of your attention and love.

You can also practice receiving what's not so easy by observing others who deal with "not so easy." At an evening speech, an audience member asks the speaker an emotionally loaded question that sends a shudder through the audience. Did you silently rail against the person's opinion? Or were you able to receive the interaction and simply sit with it? What did you learn by watching how the speaker received the question?

The Other Side of the Coin

So far the practice has been with relatively easy situations and people. But now you're about to dive into a discussion with your mate that has been historically problematic. Even so, you take a moment to acknowledge that both of you have done your best with this topic so far. Then you consider the idea that you've never done *this* before, because in truth, you haven't. You're new since the previous conversation, and so is he. Your self-promise in this fresh moment is to notice your reactions and to not fall into them. As best you can, you'll listen with acceptance (without objection or correction), and give your complete attention (you're not multitasking).

To receive your mate in this discussion is simple but not necessarily easy. Ideally, to address known trouble spots, have an agreement with your partner that if a trigger of yours (a place you usually react) comes up, you'll throw a flag on your own play. You'll stop on a dime. There's more to do after the stop, of course, but the moment you're able to call a halt to the reaction is a key turning point for the two of you.

It helps to let your partner know what you're working on and invite them to be a witness. Tell them you intend to pay attention to reactions (of yours) that send you away from kindness, respect, or love. Say that if a trigger like this happens, you'll let them know, and also that you plan to do what it takes to release it. For instance, you could disclose, "I just noticed I had a strong reaction. Let me take a moment to see what it is." Don't be in a rush to figure it all out. Get to know your reaction. What is it made of? How does it start? And then what happens next? Become aware of the steps.

Don't worry about fixing your reactions at first. Be curious instead. To allow your mate into your inner sanctum in this way is a vulnerable move, and also honest. It can bring you closer. To be a strong individual, yet voluntarily vulnerable, is loving. It's real. It's true-you.

What Is Not Receiving?

To absorb the meaning of something 100 percent, learn what it is and what it isn't. The opposite of receive is to react in opposition to the actions or words of another. A reaction is not an ultimate truth. It shows where we stand. Here's a story of two people not receiving each other. See how you relate to it. Do you recognize yourself in the story? Or a friend or partner?

Story #1

> The husband begins to speak. His wife tenses, and her shallow breathing suggests she's in fear. Her discomfort generates palpable pressure in the room. Sometimes she bristles at his words and seems anxious for her turn to speak, perhaps to set things right. The longer he speaks, the more irregular her breathing becomes. Her mouth is set, and her eyes gaze downward.
>
> Just now she listens to a story he tells, and her stare lifts briefly. Her eyes fix on him, and then suddenly they dart away. (You wonder what just happened. Did she disagree with what he said? Did she recall something terrible?) She shifts uncomfortably in her chair. Then she sits motionless, barely breathing, as if stillness will

reduce the impact of his words or make things safer. Her fingers begin to tremble, and to quiet them, she clasps her hands.

She can't hear her husband—not really. She's in her head, perhaps rehearsing a rebuttal. Or she's frozen. We don't really know. But for the moment she has traded reception, intimacy, and love for fear. Her natural wisdom is within (her inner Golden Buddha), obscured by a protective cover of defense.

He's not relaxed, either. He fights with his thoughts and fumbles his words. He treads awkwardly around the ragged edges of this difficult discussion. It's as if he's flailing in choppy waters, with a predictable storm headed his way and no life vest within reach. He has renounced his fortitude and clarity for timidity. He speaks as if he's in trouble with her—and he is. He's utterly at a loss as to how to make things better for either of them.

You've no doubt witnessed a scenario where neither partner is able to receive. Each is afraid of the other, of losing the fight, of change. Each is afraid to risk seeing themselves or the other in a loving way. To change their minds would invalidate the years of holding a firm, negative stance. They demonstrate who they learned to be. Not-him speaks to not-her. Essentially, nobody's home.

Mirror, Mirror

What we're disturbed by in another is evidence of what disturbs us about ourselves. Our evaluations of actions or words from our spouse represent our beliefs about what's important to us, and often, how we believe we should change. A client recalled words he'd said to his wife: "You seem to be willing to share a home with me, with no heart connection at all. Why do we bother? We never talk about anything meaningful!"

At some point in our discussion, though, he realized he had attributed his issue and his feelings about it to her, that the advice he offered her was better suited to him. He wasn't sharing himself freely with his wife, especially when he spoke about things he disagreed with or things that mattered. He wasn't giving her his truth or speaking from his heart. With his "aha," he began to express himself, and ask more questions. When things got testy between them, rather than surrender to frustration or trepidation, he found courage to speak. Whatever the outcome of any marriage, honest expression along the way is good practice for the health and well-being of the individuals and the relationship, or the next relationship.

Here's another story of two people who fail to receive each other. There are no details about the specific nature of their argument in order to give attention to the perfection of their nonreceiving dance. Again, see how you relate to this situation. Do you recognize yourself or your partner in any way?

Story #2

The woman casually opened the conversation. She was genuine, smart, and expressive. Her husband was a willing listener until she tossed in a point of view he considered unacceptable. Then he jumped in, determined to save them both from that intolerable thing she said.

She was devastated when he did this. How could he be so mean and thoughtless? She blamed him for her fear and shock. In her eyes, he had attacked her, and she resented him for being against her. She had done nothing to deserve such terrible treatment. She was innocent.

He felt he was a sword-ready hero, prepared to slash inaccuracies. Completely baffled about why his valiant attempts to save the day went unrecognized and unappreciated, he practiced blade flashing quite regularly, hoping to get the approval he so desperately sought. Surely someday she would celebrate his bravery, and of course she would love and admire him more. She would appreciate his protection from threats and injustices, even those generated by her.

In our work together, as she distinguished her part of the mix, she chose to alter her role. This confounded her husband. He went to great lengths to keep his warrior game alive. If there were no familiar prompts from her, he made some up in order to put his sword to work. After all, it was the game he knew. How could he relate to her without it?

The more she modified her role, the more he was left with his own issues—quite a gift! It was difficult for him to recognize, much less give up, his well-practiced habit of verbal attacks, but he did make progress. When she ultimately announced her departure, he was flat-out shocked. How could she walk away from such a well-choreographed duel? Every couple's story is a work in progress, and this story is one of those.

Before you break up as a couple, break up your patterns. Notice what you usually do and don't do that for the next day or two. To deliberately part company with a familiar, well-practiced reaction of ours wakes us up. Upheaval makes space for us—and our partner—to show up differently. Today, why not embrace the oversights, the plunders, and the falsehoods—all of them—and have a fresh discussion? You saw this in my story The Fight That Changed Everything. When I broke up my pattern in favor of a forgiving approach, everyone's behavior improved almost immediately.

Receive versus React

Being a reactor is hard on us. On top of that, if we pass our hardship to others, it creates an unfavorable ripple effect: our hardship doesn't end with us. When a sale we've worked for falls through, we're disappointed, and if we complain to friends, they feel it, too. When a new project is assigned before the last one completes, we're overwhelmed and unload our distress on those around us. When a boyfriend doesn't call, we're hurt, and we complain about it on girls' night out.

This doesn't mean we should withhold our experiences from others. It means there are options for sharing that don't burden those with whom we speak. No need to pour a hot cup of our trouble over them, or invite them into the emotional boxing ring with us. There's a way to share and work through an issue while being accountable.

One day I went out for a walk and a friend called me. With barely a hello, she launched into the details of her indignation about a recent doctor visit. In three seconds flat, my visit with nature changed from blissful to not. Yes, I answered the phone and agreed to the conversation, hoping it would contribute to the joy of my stroll. That day, the best I could do was listen to her and receive her outrage. She was full steam ahead and I didn't have the energy or inclination to stop her. I held the phone away from me and let her talk.

Another day I asked if in the future she could say, "I'm upset and need to talk. Is now a good time?" This would give me the option to delay it. "May I tell you about this incident, so I can see my way to a solution?" would also be a great way to take responsibility and ask for permission to talk.

Examine the Consequences

To investigate the impact of a reaction within yourself, take three steps.

1. Take a moment to state aloud a strong reaction of yours, and then name the emotion.

   "My sister is greedy and wants all the jewelry from my mother's estate." (I'm feeling resentful.)

"My husband ignores me. Why can't we have a conversation when I need one? Is that so hard?" (I'm feeling angry.)

"I'm a terrible organizer. What's wrong with me?" (I'm being self-critical, unloving to myself.)

2. Notice that strong negative thoughts show up somewhere in you, and they cause a stress response. What is the sensation, and where is it—in your heart? Head? Solar plexus?

3. Take a look at how stress has affected you over time. Do you have physical symptoms that correlate with stress? Here's how traditional medicine chimes in.

The American Institute of Stress notes fifty signs and symptoms that indicate stress, such as headaches, jaw clenching, difficulty concentrating, or racing thoughts.[26] Healthline names eleven signs of stress, including acne, chronic pain, frequent sickness, decreased energy, insomnia, changes in sex drive, digestive and appetite changes, depression, rapid heartbeat, and excess sweating.[27] The Mayo Clinic suggests solutions such as regular physical activity, relaxation techniques, keeping a sense of humor, visits with family and friends, and time for hobbies or personally pleasurable activities.[28]

Mind and body are a team. When we think a stressful thought, our body matches it with a stress response. In our youth we don't consider the impact of negative emotions because our bodies have beautifully designed recovery systems. But the longer we live, the more the physical effects of anxious thoughts seem to catch up with us.

What About a Chill Pill?

Do we have the ability to dump a worrisome thought at the curb and walk away? We do. We can turn our attention to the next thing on our to-do list. We can pet the cat. We can admire buds bursting on the forsythia or listen to an uplifting podcast on a hike. Any of these actions helps, temporarily, but at some point we must face ourselves. We must meet our stressful reaction and ask it to speak. What is it afraid of? Or worried about? A stressful thought can lead us to a positive recognition of something we need.

The larger question for many of us is not "can I give up my reaction?" but "should I?" It seems appropriate to have feisty opinions about how the world can run better, how clean the oceans should be, or what constitutes a healthy meal. Isn't speaking up a good thing? It is. But what if you could be you, spunk and all, with one simple change: be extra aware of sensations in your body as you speak.

Be in your body *and* express yourself. Pay attention to your legs, feet, and hips while telling a woe-is-me story to friends over dinner. Check in with your neck and shoulders as you listen to national news. To pay heed to the miracle of feedback from your physical body and to honor those reports is worth your time and attention. Your organs experience what you think, say, and do. Your body is your most intimate partner.

At some point in my marriage, I recognized that my automatic reactions hindered me in a significant way, that being a reactor didn't help *me*, or *him*, or *us*. Gradually, two things gained importance instead: being awake and being in love. Being awake meant to be aware of my reactions but not become them. The second part, being in love, didn't mean being breathlessly head over heels with Eric, but rather, that my priority was to embody love. Even in difficulty, I preferred to stand in love, to make love the foundation of my life expression. This was true-me, the me I knew myself to be, and it engendered a profound inner commitment.

Frustration with Someone Else's Frustration

In my relationship with Eric, we discovered a helpful guideline around reactions. When we were upset, the person in the best shape volunteered to listen to the other. If neither of us was in decent shape, we postponed the interaction.

One of Eric's income sources was the sale of used pro audio gear on eBay. When sales were great, he was happy. When sales flatlined, he became grumpy and blamed eBay policy makers for one thing or another. When there were shipping difficulties such as damaged boxes, he complained that UPS was surely heaving packages marked fragile against a brick wall. His trouble was someone else's fault.

I wondered: if I could receive his blameful communication, how might that help me or him? Could hearing him make a positive difference? Because I was in the best shape (in those eBay situations), my choice was to be the listener. At first, however, I couldn't really hear his upset. Below are steps that helped me "get right" with myself (learn how to stand in love) so I could receive him and his strong frustration.

A. I began to listen to Eric about his eBay issues as if he were not my guy. He was an irritated male in another woman's life. Because his customer service problems didn't relate to me, there was nothing to fix. This was my first step, simply because no other step seemed emotionally available to me. This got things moving, though, which was important.

B. As time progressed, it became possible to make peace with the fact that this was not some mystery guy, this was Eric. This was the man in my bed. This was the man who held my hand at the movies and went on hikes with me. Little by little, I let his rants come closer, to test whether I could accept "what is." Could I be with his setbacks, his feelings of being thwarted, and do nothing about it?

C. Once I could be with his agitation, my next step was to walk toward "What if he's not against me, he's for me?" And then "What if he's trying to do something good—and what would that be?" One day, my spontaneous response was to smile at him during his tirade and say, "You know, I don't thank you enough for all the trouble you go through to put food on the table and money in the bank. It's hard sometimes. Thank you for all of this."

Eric stopped. He fell silent and sat down on a nearby chair. I gave him my complete attention, and said nothing more. After a minute he responded, "You're welcome." Then he rose from his seat, picked up the tattered box with the damaged equipment, and began to solve his shipping problem. In future situations, he was calmer about eBay difficulties. When he did get upset, it didn't last long. If I was around, he'd glance over at me with a look that said, "Yeah. I know. I get it." And then he simply shifted gears.

- Did Eric make this change himself? He did. I assisted.
- What did it cost me to help him? It cost me an old habit that I didn't want anyway. I gave up being frustrated in response to his frustration.
- Did I get to a better place by witnessing the good in his sales and shipping efforts? Yes.
- Did he get to a better place by realizing the good in his efforts? Absolutely.

Two people got better because one person walked toward love. This is what partners who care about each other and who care about how their hearts feel at the end of the day can do for each other. The possibility of a more peaceful world truly begins with two people who work out an eBay shipping problem.

Each time we set aside ingrained reactions and choose to receive, love leads us toward ease. There, our connection is more intimate. You'll also notice an uptick in something you value, such as vitality, happiness, or creativity. When my protest energy was freed up for new purposes, my writing came forward. That was a happy surprise, one I appreciate daily.

What will rise up in you when you react less and receive more?

~~~~~

It always seems impossible until it's done.
—Nelson Mandela

17

Conversation: Be Impossible to Argue With

ACCORDING TO RELATIONSHIP researcher John Gottman, four main actions kill a relationship: criticism, contempt, defensiveness, and stonewalling. Couples who argue practice most of these in one fell swoop. Next is a dialogue with a comedian who is weary of arguments with his wife. He believes she is the reason for the stress in their relationship, that what's wrong with them is all about her. What a great place to begin, since this is the usual starting line for couples who have fallen out of love. Each is certain the other is at fault for the condition of the relationship.

The phone session with him covered more than a couple of core skills, but for clarity and simplicity, here is the part of the conversation that emphasizes breathe and receive. I'll bold these core skills in the text.

~~~~~

After an initial catch-up, he opens up about his circumstances. He grouses about his wife and his career and declares that he's officially bottomed out. He concedes that he has no idea what to do.

ME: Okay. Ready or not, here we go.

He laughs. Clearly, he's ready to roll!

ME: First, even though you don't like your wife right now, you're a match to her. Do you know that?

HIM: What do you mean? I'm a bitch?

Oh, yeah, there's his sense of humor!

ME: I hear you. Do you know that you treat her the way you treat yourself?

HIM: Well, what do you mean by *that*?!?

He's laughing in an achy-breaky, please take me out of my misery kind of way.

ME: If you're not sure how you treat yourself, listen to how you speak to her aloud, silently, or under your breath. You'll have your answer in no time.

The performer in him speaks in accents, and now he becomes a tough mafia hit man with a thick tongue.

HIM [as the mafia man]: Well, that's not gonna be too good!

ME: So do you really know what I'm talking about?

HIM [still a hit man]: Keep talkin'.

ME: I'm saying, "mirror, mirror on the wall." Your relationship with her reflects your relationship with yourself. Any trouble you think you have with her is actually trouble you have with yourself.

HIM: Oh, I don't think so.

ME: How 'bout if I give you an example of how this works?

HIM: I dare you.

Which makes me laugh out loud. I love working with this man. You'll note my directness with him as we work. We've done sessions before, and I know him well. No soft shoe approach with this guy. He responds best to straightforward, bold statements.

ME: Do you pay attention to things like: What am I saying to her? How is my tone? How does she respond? Do you consider these questions?

HIM: Nope. I'm too pissed.

ME: I get it. Do you see the wisdom of attention to such questions?

HIM: You can't use me and "wisdom" in the same sentence. I'm not sure if I can pay attention to how I say things to her or how she responds. I'm too pissed.

ME: Are you too pissed right now?

HIM: No.

ME: So is it okay if we look at this now?

HIM: Yes.

ME: When you're not happy, and you talk with her, what happens?

HIM: Pretty soon she's not happy either.

ME: And why is that?

HIM: I affect her.

ME: Sure. If we put your life up on a screen to study it, we'd see the story that you're in pain, and you share it. You pour pain from your pitcher into her glass. What does she do?

HIM: She drinks what I poured.

ME: And now there are two people in pain. She doesn't like that. And why would she? She doesn't want to be the woman she becomes when you're upset. That's not who she is.

> *I wait. When he takes a long breath over the phone, we continue.*

ME: If you don't love *you*, how can you possibly love *her*? I mean, think about it. To love someone else, you must know firsthand what love is. Does that make sense to you?

HIM: Yeah…

> *We take time to speak of slow moves and small steps. We discuss how it's impossible to leap from "I hate you" to "I love you," to paste a smile on your face and say words that will improve things in an instant. We explore what it takes to build a connection. I mention a line from a Rumi poem, "Out beyond ideas of wrongdoing and rightdoing, there is a field. I'll meet you there."[29] I encourage him to find his way to that field.*

HIM: All of that makes sense. [He takes a long pause.] My wife and I have so, SO far to go.

Self-Talk

ME: Ask me a question.

HIM: Go back closer to the beginning. What do I do first?

ME: First, take a deep **breath**. Get calm, cool, and collected. Then don your lab coat. Be a scientist and study how you relate to her, which also shows how you relate to yourself, and how you speak to yourself. Shall we investigate your self-talk?

HIM: Oh, self-talk. That's not good. I can tell you that.

ME: It's where we all begin. First, put your attention on what you say. For instance, wake up and observe when you're in the middle of self-criticism.

We have a silly moment where we talk about how he wallows in self-criticism and then slathers her with it.

HIM: Right now, yes, I'm slathering her.

ME: This change you desire is a big job, so why not break it down into tiny pieces? Where might you start?

HIM: Ugh. How do you eat an elephant? One bite at a time. I don't know how to eat this elephant. What did you do?

ME: For one entire sunrise to sunset, I observed my thoughts. I was so shocked by my discoveries that I made the decision to practice noticing my thoughts for two weeks straight. [He howls about my story.] Shall I tell you what happened exactly?

HIM: I'm on the edge of my seat.

ME: Each time I noticed a self-critical or negative thought, I said something short, sweet, and simple:

> "Oh, hello, I see you."
> "Huh. I'm being critical."
> "Ah. Negative thought."

When I was alone, I spoke aloud whenever possible. I recommend that. I had no idea what was going on in my mind because I hadn't been paying attention!

HIM: Well, that assignment will be pretty overwhelming, because that's all I do. I beat up on myself.

ME: I understand. Tell me this first step and let's see if you've got it.

HIM: Pay attention to what I'm thinking. Notice negative thoughts. Say something to myself when I see one, like "hello there."

ME: Exactly. Ready for step two? [He agrees.] Take your attention from that self-critical thought and put it on something that gives you a little relief. Find a thought that calms you or offers a pat on the back. Make statements like:

> "Oh, good for me. I noticed."
> "This is okay. I'm learning…"
> "Yay! I took a small step. I noticed my thought…"

So practice observation of your thoughts, and when you're good at that, interrupt the negative thoughts and add a dash of relief.

HIM: Okay, I'll practice and call you again in a few days.

> *It seemed this would conclude our conversation, and the assignment gave him plenty to do. But he went on to tell another story about a serious argument with his wife, one that began when he described his plans for a career move. She protested. He defended.*

> *She finally said, "You don't even believe in this yourself! You're trying to sell both of us on this idea!" She insisted he wasn't ready to give up his day job and become a full-time comedian. She was sure they couldn't swing it financially.*

> *Again, he defended. "No, that's not true. I'm ready. And we can totally do this." He went on to tell her all the reasons why she was flat-out wrong. Needless to say, things didn't turn out well. Neither of them was open to incoming information.*

> *This is how any argument gains traction! Nobody **receives**! And then, before you know it, the woman becomes a person she*

doesn't enjoy—doesn't even recognize—and the man becomes someone for whom he has no respect. There's a better way! We continue the conversation because he asked for more.

HIM: My wife and I argue *all the time.* We drop bombs on each other. It gets out of control.

ME: Tell me what you want.

HIM: Oh, gawd…to stop fighting so much.

ME: Well, this is another big job. Another elephant. How might you take some small steps?

HIM: Here's how I'm stuck. I tell my wife I want to change my career, but she doesn't listen. She tells me I'm wrong. Then what? You would advise me to listen to her, I'm sure. But I don't want to listen to her.

ME: Tell me more about that.

HIM: Her words are an onslaught. [He switches to an Italian accent.] I say to her, "HEY! Slow down! I'm drownin' here!"

What Does It Mean Exactly—Breathe and Receive?

ME: This is the part where you take a deep **breath** to slow things down. What would allow you to **receive** her?

HIM: Maybe I could say to her, "Hold on there, can you give me one piece at a time. Small bites, please."

ME: That could totally work. Take a deep **breath.** Listen to her response. **Receive** her. Really hear her point of view, even if you've heard it before, or think you have. By the way, her feedback—is it a threat to you?

HIM: Well, I don't like the idea that she can threaten me, but yeah...

ME: What if she's not threatening you but simply stating thoughts and concerns?

HIM: What she says makes me uptight.

ME: Is it possible that how you *interpret* her words is what scares you?

HIM [in the voice of one of his frilly, silly comedy characters]: Oh, you mean I'm scaring myself?

ME: You're the only person who can scare you.

HIM: Well, when she talks, I feel pressured.

ME: Let's look at your interpretation of what she says.

> *We speak at length about his specific interpretations and concerns. One is the feeling that he can't move unless she says "jump." He doesn't feel "he's his own man."*

ME: So...if you're feeling out of sorts, scared, trapped...what might you do?

HIM: You'd suggest that I **breathe** about it.

ME: It's an excellent first step. Meet your fear, recognize it, **breathe** about it. Investigate "I'm uptight." [We talk about the practical how-to aspects of this.] Then what?

HIM: So many pop quizzes! I don't remember the next step. Maybe listen to her?

ME: That's it. **Receive** her. Concentrate to make sure you really understand her communication. To hear her doesn't signify your agreement, or that you must do what she says.

HIM: Wait. I don't have to *do* anything with what she says? Just listen and make sure I understand her point? This would be highly unusual on my part, I must tell you.

ME: Yes, it would shatter an old pattern of yours, wouldn't it? Can you see how this could help if you wish to change things with her? To **breathe** deeply and **receive** someone's communication is a new move for any couple who argues. Take your time with this part. Can you tell me what you might say to encourage her to talk? Or how you might remind yourself to listen?

HIM: Oh God. I don't have any idea. I don't do either of those.

ME: How about the basic idea "tell me more"?

HIM: As in, "Please tell me more about why you're upset?" That's the opposite of what I do.

ME: True. But here's the secret. The more you offer the "tell me more" invitation to yourself, the more genuinely you'll be able to say it to her.

> *We discuss ways he might learn to explore his thoughts more often, get to know himself, and to grow a kinder foundation within. The more he appreciates himself, the more he can offer that to his wife. She will feel appreciated as well. (This exploration will continue in his future sessions.)*

ME: When you've heard her communication, check to see if she's done. Has she shared what's on her mind and heart? Ask her: "Is there anything else you want to say about this? Is there something you think I might not know about this…?" Invite her to empty.

HIM [repeating the statement]: "Is there something you think I might not know about this?"

ME: Once she shares what's on her mind, let her know you heard her. Be real. I'm talking about simple statements such as "That makes sense to me." Some others would be:

"I can understand how you would think that."

"I get it. I thought about that, too."

"Let me see if I've got this..." Then retell her points, her side of the story.

See how you do with these simple statements. And when she's done speaking, instead of pouncing on her words or defending your point of view, **breathe**...and **receive.** Thank her.

HIM: All right. I get it. This is so different from what I do now.

ME: The first time you try to **receive** her, you may be able to do it beautifully. Or you may yell. We don't know. Give yourself room to try and fail. Is that a deal?

HIM: Okay. Deal.

ME: And once you've absorbed her point of view, sit with it. Then see what's there for you to say. "Thank you for all of that. I'm glad to know where you stand about my possible career change. May I tell you a few more things from my side?" Do you need her permission to say more? No, of course not. But to ask for permission opens the way for her to say, "Yes, please. Tell me your thoughts." It lights up the *receiving* road in her heart. Now you've got two people **receiving**. It's a simple, brilliant thing to do in a conversation. Because you heard her and she was able to express from her heart, she'll hear you better.

HIM: OMG. We have such a long way to go.

ME: You have some focused work ahead of you. It's a good thing your job is simple.

HIM: Okay. I'll pay attention. **Breathe. Receive.** Thanks, I'll talk to you in a few days.

~~~~~

Even if you're a couple who argues often, you can shift this over time. There are two basic ways partners can listen, and they have opposite outcomes. When a couple listens to each other using the filter "I agree, or I disagree," neither of them learns anything new. In the end, each keeps the beliefs that maintain the standoff, with little chance of feeling closer or more understood.

But there's another way: learn about each other. This requires open questions such as "What's important to you about this?" or "How do you see this working?" Coming up with questions that are authentic for you is key. When a couple listens in this way, it's possible to find common ground. Then a problem brings two people closer and even reminds them why they got together.

If you and your partner are stuck in a persistent disagreement, here's an exercise you might try. Find a time when both of you are rested, fed, and calm. Schedule a friendly debate where you trade viewpoints. You take your partner's point of view, and your partner takes yours. For a prescribed amount of time (ten minutes works well) sing the praises of the perspective you resist. Use a timer. When your ten minutes are up, communicate what you now understand that you didn't previously, and offer possible solutions based on your new comprehension. Next your partner does the same. See where the exercise leads you.

Disagreements bring us closer if they are used to create breathing room. When we give attention to our partner and say, "Tell me more," it turns out that we are able to express more, too. How ironic, how profound, that to receive another opens the way for our own expression.

~~~~~

A great marriage is not when the "perfect couple" comes together.
It is when an imperfect couple learns to enjoy their differences.
—Dave Meurer

18

Core Skill #3: Observe

THE ABILITY TO observe is vital to any healthy relationship because it supports conscious change. Without this skill, we unwittingly recycle habits, including some that are detrimental. To observe is to step out of a situation, to hold it less personally and examine what was said or done with curiosity, as if viewing someone else. This is not difficult, though it is a clear distinction from what many of us do.

It can seem counterintuitive to back up to examine ourselves or odd that to take a close look means stepping away. We are not accustomed to being curious bystanders, either, with a friendly pen and notepad to survey ourselves. Human beings, especially smart and talented ones, need reminders to observe playfully, to opt for lighthearted note-taking, rather than self-critical.

Observation discloses how we move through our day. How do we relate to others when we're happy? Fearful? Or when we're angry? A step back from a spat makes it possible to view the emotional buttons on display. Rather than react and repeat, we can observe, which heightens awareness and keeps the focus and responsibility on ourselves. After all, our buttons are *our* buttons. Other people show us where they are and where our work is, and what a service they provide!

Stepping back to observe also reminds us that we're in a physical body, yet we have the capacity to be the watcher of our actions. To distinguish who we are from what we do emphasizes that we're more than our emotions, our personality, and our beliefs. We are spirits-in-residence. We are eternal spirits housed in skin. In the words of systems theorist and futurist R. Buckminster Fuller, "Ninety-nine percent of who you are is invisible and untouchable."

Living with spirit awareness generates spaciousness.

Start at the Beginning

To understand how observation works, choose a situation that is utterly insignificant. If you attempt to observe yourself in a complicated emotional standoff, you'll become confused and give up. Instead, select a circumstance that matters not one iota.

Here's one: I'm cooking in the kitchen, and a man calls on the landline. He ordered some audio equipment from my husband but hasn't yet received it. I feel mildly bothered by this. Why didn't he call Eric's cell? Why didn't Eric answer the phone? The caller's complaint makes me wish I'd ignored the ring. All of this happens in a few seconds. The moment is nothing—not important in the least. It's over quickly with no lasting effects. What a perfect time to practice being an observer of myself. Remember, I'm observing as if I'm not me, so I'll refer to myself as *her* and *she*. I'll ask questions and state the facts of what happened (aloud if possible).

> How were the first few seconds of the phone call? What was her attitude (meaning my attitude)? What did she feel? Did her attitude vary as she spoke? How did her reaction(s) affect her body? Where in her body did she sense emotions? How did the caller respond? How did the call end?

Being affirmative about the findings of your observation will encourage you to continue to examine with those kind eyes of yours. Speak in casual, forgiving ways: "Oh, look what she did!" Or "Good for her—what a strong reaction that was!" If you're pulled into self-criticism, just fall back and give it another go later, or perhaps choose a different situation altogether.

Next—Harder Stuff

When you're ready to observe situations that carry more emotion, continue to follow the basic protocol. Stay simple, and tell the story as if it's not about you. Put it up on a mental screen. Report facts only. Here's an example.

What happened?

> A woman offered her husband a margarita. He said "no, thank you" and walked to the kitchen to get a glass of water. There he saw $100 worth of liquor—gin, vodka, tequila—on the counter, purchased that day.

Then what happened?

> The liquor and the receipt shocked him. Yesterday she told him she didn't have money to pay a household bill.

How did he feel?

> He felt confused. In disbelief. He was upset that she opted to buy booze rather than pay the utility company.

What did he notice in his body?

> His body tensed, and he held his breath. Hot energy rose up through him, and his face flushed.

Did he come to any conclusions?

> He concluded that her judgment was wrong, that finances should go first toward essentials. A few hours

later, he wondered, "Is it so terrible to live with me that she must drown her feelings?"

Anything else?

The next day he discovered that she had ordered a couple of cases of wine in addition, so the total spent was four times the original amount.

Observation is a dispassionate look at an event. Each simple question opens the door for factual answers. This helps us move from being upset to being neutral, in the direction of love as the foundation for future conversations.

How Dreams Help Us Observe

While dreams are not the predominant way we observe ourselves, they deserve an honorable mention and a story. Dreams can offer potent assistance, especially if they furnish a fresh view of things the next day.

During the last months of Eric's cancer, I was exhausted, emotionally drained, and worried. My desire was to feel calmer, but I didn't know how. Even when others stepped in to care for him, many tasks fell to me, and I was overwhelmed. On top of all that, a mountain of grief had welled up in me about the day I would wake up without him. Pulling blankets over me one evening at bedtime, I prayed for a good night's sleep and a fresh start in the morning. "There has to be a better way," I thought. That night, I had a vivid, colorful dream.

My girlfriend and I had performed menial jobs all day in a restaurant. We felt the heat and bustle of a hectic kitchen and heard the sounds of cooks hollering and pots and pans banging. On the way out the door after work, Tammy and I felt satisfied but had no desire to repeat those same efforts the next day.

Our conversation shifted to how we might enjoy a change of pace, and Tammy said, "Hang on, I'll be right back." She pointed to a spot where I should wait for her, then reappeared in a tiny red convertible sports car. I wondered how she'd gotten so small.

The convertible top had two layers, black and red, which I lifted to enter the car, and then I became mini, too. One layer fitted to my face like cloth and allowed me to see and breathe perfectly. When I drew the second layer to me, both layers disappeared, and we seemed life-size again. With this, the landscape became otherworldly beautiful! We were so happy to step out of hard work into a breathtaking view of things!

There was no wind, not even a sensation of air moving across our faces. We scaled a few impressive hills, and then she offered to demonstrate how fast the car would go. After the initial burst of speed, we moved in what felt like slow motion, except there was no limit to how far or how quickly we could travel.

Bright vistas of color, light, and rolling hills surrounded us. Pristine views of increasing beauty unfolded as we drove, each scene more splendid than the previous. Peering over the edge of the convertible, I saw our tires riding on carpets of lavender flowers without leaving tracks!

As we approached the most colorful view of all, Tammy attempted an aerial flip with the car. We tried several times, but it didn't work, and caused us to laugh. "No problem," she said. "I'll get out of the car and teach you how to flip all by yourself."

Upon awakening, I reflected on the initial perspective in the dream: hard work, noise, and effort at the restaurant. The moment Tammy and I resolved to have a little fun, things changed. We enjoyed striking views and a world of extraordinary beauty. We felt calm and expressed delight and awe as we drove. Same day, two radically different views.

That morning with Eric, I became a red-sports-car-caretaker. Dish washing and food preparation morphed into slow-motion pleasure. Bliss poured from me as I made his bed, helped him change clothes, or drove to the store for an item he needed. My attention drifted to the sound of my steps, to the beat of my heart. While opening a stuck window, I felt my arm muscles pull together to lift the sill. The sound of the broomcorn bristles sweeping across our leaf-covered sidewalk seemed musical. A calm enveloped me.

Following the dream, I was less worried about Eric and more peaceful about my future. Even when he struggled in pain, it was easier to stand next to him and offer my hands, my legs, my love. Perhaps I could support his path after all. Maybe there was a way to live without him, to stay behind and somehow be all right. Maybe, just maybe, my actions could comfort him on the journey to his new state of being. Together we could drive on a carpet of lavender flowers.

Think of all the ways life offers avenues to observe ourselves—and then, if we choose, we can soften our perspective, or open it. We can relinquish stress in favor of astonishing views. We can feel our way through duties or assignments with awareness. We can relax as we move forward.

If you have a new-to-me grasp of what this core skill of observation involves, that it is a step out of the fray in order to see details close up, you're in a just right place. The trio—breathe, receive, and observe— grows our emotional intelligence. All three profoundly affect the quality of how we engage with our day. Being an observer helps us realize that we're both a masterpiece and a work in progress, simultaneously.

~~~~~

> There is nothing in a caterpillar that tells
> you it's going to be a butterfly.
> —R. Buckminster Fuller

19

Conversation: Will You Help Me When I Get Old?

THIS COUPLE'S CONVERSATION illustrates the beginning steps of observation and how your own learning curve might progress at first. These two have been married five years; it's the second marriage for both. Their requested focus for this session is to "make it through a day without getting tripped up by each other." Observation is a new concept for both partners, and I'll offer narration throughout the exchange to make it easy to learn along with them.

Mouse-in-the-Corner is a way of working with couples that I developed over the years, and it is used in the upcoming session. In Mouse-in-the-Corner, one partner temporarily steps out of active participation in the conversation to observe, quiet as a mouse. This partner offers silence with presence. Of course, both people agree in advance to its use.

Here are some details about how it works and why I use it.

- **Mouse-in-the-Corner creates safe space.** One partner can speak truth without the other jumping all over it. This is especially helpful with partners who interrupt or argue.
- **Mouse-in-the-Corner provides two kinds of learning.** For the partner who speaks, it is a supervised occasion to own their truth. The quiet partner learns to receive.

- **Mouse-in-the-Corner creates trust between me and both clients through full transparency.** When a husband attends a session for the first time at the invitation of his wife, I often set it up so that he watches me work with her while he's Mouse-in-the-Corner. This allows him to observe that I don't favor her. He sees firsthand that he'll be treated with fairness, which relaxes him. When it's his turn, he'll speak without hesitation. This way of working brings out the best in both partners. Of course, if a husband brings his wife to his session, she'll be introduced to the process this way as well. The use of Mouse-in-the-Corner lends particular power in situations where the silent partner witnesses the unraveling of a trouble spot but doesn't get blamed.
- **Mouse-in-the-Corner creates trust between partners.** Both individuals learn things they never knew about the other. When each hears a side of the story they had never considered, it is a reminder that other worthy perspectives exist. The privilege of listening fosters a broader playing field for both people.

The conversation with this couple shows the magnetic force of patterns. You'll watch them argue in favor of the past. You'll get a feel for Mouse-in-the-Corner and how it bids a steep learning curve. You'll be reminded that change is almost never a one-shot thing. References to core skills will be in bold.

~~~~~

ME: Are you two getting along so well I've lost my job?

HER: Well, not so fast there!

HIM: I think we're getting better at smoothing over riffs, or at least we see them coming. We had a few riffs over the weekend.

ME [to both of them]**:** Who would like to fill me in on what happened?

HER: We were joking that I should help him with a test his doctor had requested. We were having fun with it, using different accents and attitudes back and forth, acting silly. Then suddenly the conversation changed. It took a drastic turn.

HIM: Things changed when I asked her if she would help me someday when I'm old and decrepit. She said she would, but refused to help me with the test I had to do right now. So I pressed a little about our later years when we have to assist each other with health issues. I really wanted to know if she would be there for me. It took a while, but she finally said she would. [He leans back in his chair, satisfied.]

HER: It was troublesome for me when his tone shifted. He looked at me in an accusatory way, with the attitude that I might not be there to help him in his old age. We went from having a really good time to "what the hell happened?"

[She turns to address him directly.] You don't think I'm going to take care of you?!? You took a bazooka and shot me back to when I helped my first husband through his illness and his death. Where I went was "How can you say that?!?" I've been there. I've done that. I know all about that. Don't you dare question me!

[She is really emotional now and turns back to me.] I got upset that he could think for one second that I wouldn't help him. I helped my first husband, and also helped my mother and my dad. I've been with sick and dying people way more than he has. But he didn't back off. I got stone-cold quiet. Here we were, getting ready for a lovely day of golf with friends. This argument was not how I wanted to start my day. To rein in all my emotions as I got into the car, I said, "We have to talk about this—later!"

HIM: I never knew how she jumped in for all these people in her past. Once I understood, that dialed it back for me.

ME: Thank you. May I work with her first to see where it takes us?

*He nods and goes into Mouse-in-the-Corner. We've discussed this before, and he knows his job is to **observe** and not bring attention to himself. If he has questions, he'll ask them later.*

ME [to her]: Does that work for you as well? [She nods.] Let's talk about how you took his actions personally, that you heard his inquiry as an attack on your character.

HER: Yes, it did feel like an attack, and I did take it personally.

ME: Would you like to talk about how you might work with this sort of thing, maybe how to soften it?

HER: Yes, I'm ready.

Is He "For Me" or "Against Me"?

ME: If he loves you…and he does something that hurts your feelings… maybe he's not actually doing what you think he's doing. Logic would tell us that his intention would never be to hurt you. Is this an idea you'd like to look into?

HER: But if this man loves me, why does he treat me like this? You don't treat someone you love the way he treated me.

*Welcome to the great privilege of **observing** someone. This woman is an ideal student because she has objections. Right out of the gate, her response to my suggestion "maybe he's not doing what you think he's doing" speaks a thousand words. Instead of **receiving** that idea—considering it—what does she do? She states what she's always done. She's not quick to agree to self-**observation**. She's sure she knows what he did and why he should not have done it.*

ME: What was your point of view about what he said?

HER: What? What are you saying?

ME: What was your reaction to his question about being there for him when he gets old and decrepit?

> *Can you tell? I'm asking her to step back from her upset to* ***observe***. *In order to answer me, she must move out of her reaction enough to see that she had one. She's having trouble with that. It's okay. This is how it goes when we begin to learn how we relate. Her face has a blank look in response to my query, so I offer a more specific question.*

ME: Was your husband *for you* or *against you?*

HER: He was against me.

> *Her response says a lot, doesn't it? I'll ask her a series of questions about the logic of her conclusion (that he was against her).*

ME: Does he love you?

HER: Yes.

ME: Does he care about you?

HER: Yes.

ME: Does he look out for you?

HER: Yes.

ME: So, on principle, can you describe how he might be against you?

HER: But that's what I thought.

Facts Versus Interpretation

ME: True. But now we have a new moment. Let's look again. Together. What occurred? Can you tell me some facts?

My request is to look back and report facts, but as you'll note, she evaluates the situation instead. This is an important distinction.

HER: He hurt my feelings. He made a mistake.

ME: That isn't actually what happened. That he made a mistake is a conclusion, not a fact. An example of a fact would be stating the words he said and then the words of your response.

HER: Oh, I see. He said, "Will you help me when I get old?" and I said, "How dare you question me?" I got riled up.

ME: Exactly. Those are facts. Then you drew a conclusion. What was your conclusion?

HER: That he made a mistake.

ME: Precisely. Now that the facts are stated, are you willing to consider other possible conclusions, as in, "What else could I have decided from those facts?"

HER: I don't think I came to an inaccurate conclusion. I think what I think.

She's not buying. I try another approach.

ME: Okay, let's review. Fair enough?

HER: Fair enough.

ME: First you reacted negatively to his tone of voice, and you took his question personally. He doesn't love you if he's asking *that* question. Right?

HER: Yes.

ME: Then you decided he's against you.

HER: Yes. I believed that then and still believe it now.

ME: What if that's not true? What if he's not against you? Is that possible?

> *I'm looking for evidence of her flexibility. She'll need it going forward.*

HER: Okay. Wow. Well, I didn't even consider that. Not at all. I didn't ask myself that question. It would never occur to me that my conclusion was wrong.

> *Let's pause for a deep **breath** here and **receive** what she said. Consider her statement: "It would never occur to me that my conclusion was wrong." Have you ever been so sure of yourself that you instantly dismissed conclusions besides yours? No doubt we could all use help with opening our perspective.*

ME: What if you consistently made the assumption that he's *for you?* The only question on the table would be "How is he for me this time?"

> *There's a long pause here. She gazes at my eyes intently, as if her brain may possibly explode.*

ME: What if he is *for you*…and furthermore, what if he's *for the two of you?*

> *I'm going slowly here, hoping to facilitate the brain explosion. Still no words from her.*

ME: And maybe…he doesn't know how to express that he's *for you* and *for the two of you* in a way that you understand.

I lean in her direction to check in more closely. She's quiet—in thought.

I wait a little longer, then ask how she's doing.

HER: Just listening…

I Do What I've Always Done

ME: Rather than assume he's trying to inflict hurt, or even that he's being careless, is it possible he's offering an honest question about taking care of him when he's old? Is it possible he's revealing an insecurity?

HER: I would never think the way you suggest. I get offended pretty often.

ME: Would you prefer to look for good in his actions?

HER: Yes, but I'm not sure I can. I'd like to.

ME: Do you know where you might start?

HER: Not really. No…

> *We have perfectly good reasons to stay the same. With too many unknowns or no guarantees of success, we often decide to stay parked right where we are.*

ME: When he spouts something you disagree with, or find offensive, or hurtful, what is your reaction? [I'm asking her to **observe**.]

HER: I kind of jump all over him and assume he's being an asshole or inconsiderate or whatever.

> *You know, right here I want to stand up and do the hula. Her tone is suddenly one of discovery. She's not serious about how she's right and he's wrong. She's saying, "Oh, look at me!*

*I see what I do." This is an example of how **observation** is about facts, not fault.*

ME: Well, good for you, to recognize that! Do you want to take a look at this view that "he's an asshole, he's inconsiderate" or do you want to leave it alone?

Get ready for her answer. She's not giving up old ways yet.

HER: Gosh, I do what I've always done. I don't know how to be different. I think my reaction is my reaction, and that's that. It's how I am. And maybe always will be?

ME: Maybe. It's your call.

*She's like so many of us. We repeat what we do, even though it doesn't work and we know it. This is where **observation** can highlight a pattern and a consequence. It makes them both clear. For now I love that she recognizes what she currently does. And remember: her husband, quiet as a mouse, listens to every word.*

HER: Well, I don't like how it's going with us. I'd like this aspect of our relationship to change.

ME: What's your plan? What will you do about this?

HER: I don't know what to do about it. He's got to stop the questions.

ME: Oh, good luck with that!

HER: No, really. Let's get him to stop questioning me. Shouldn't we talk to him now?

ME: You can change him?

HER: It would be easier, right?

ME: I know it seems that way. But if you want a different result, what might you do?

HER: You're going to suggest that I change what I do.

ME: Are you up for that?

HER: I think so.

She's hesitant. We're not ready to move forward yet.

ME: Please tell me a little more about you and change.

HER: I understand change is possible. I just don't know if I can do it. Am I capable? That's where I'm a little stuck.

She actually stated this hesitancy before but I forgot about it, so here it is again. I love how this works. She and I are partners here, and she reminded me of important information she gave me earlier.

ME: That makes sense. Right now you have little confidence that you can change this. When you altered something about your life in the past, did you know that you could?

HER: No, not really, not until it changed. Then I knew.

We take time here to remember and reinforce her competency. We cite specific examples from her past where she initiated change and was successful, and we speak of these experiences in detail. This is a key piece of this process, and it takes some time. After the review, her confidence rises.

ME: You've never made this change before. There are no guarantees. Your experiment might fail. Are you willing to use your strengths and skills, the ones we spoke about just now, in this current situation?

HER: You know, thank you for asking me to look at my past and remember the ways I've already done this. I have the skills. This is important to me.

ME: This change you desire is entirely up to you. What your husband does is his business. Agreed?

HER: Yes, I get it.

ME: Let's return to an earlier question. What if your husband is not even doing what you think he's doing? What if your interpretation of him is inaccurate?

> *This is a deliberate backtrack to see if anything that didn't make sense some minutes ago makes sense now. You never know. Maybe a new comprehension clicked into place.*

HER: Well, but I'm so sure I'm right. I do what I do because I have good reason for doing it.

ME: Does this work for you and for the partnership?

HER: It doesn't. But what he says seems like a personal affront, directed at me and not too nice to me. So he should stop that, right?

> *Even with her renewed confidence about making changes, she returns to her default point of view: change him. This is how we may progress—two steps forward, one step back. We feel brave enough to consider a change but wave it off and go back to where we were.*

ME: May I offer a possible starting place for this new approach?

HER: Please.

Learning to Observe—First Steps

ME: The first step is to notice your reaction. When you recognize it, say, "Oh, I'm having a reaction." And why do that? Then you're not in the reaction so much. The reaction is over there where you can point to it, and examine it, as an **observer**. Do you know what I mean?

HER: A little. This is a new idea to me. I don't usually separate my reaction from me at all. I didn't know you could do that. Or should do that. It sounds weird, actually.

ME: The idea here is that if you're not in your reaction, you have options.

HER: But I believe in my reaction. I'm sure I'm correct.

ME: And therefore nothing shifts. The problem continues. You changed nothing.

HER: Right... So I have a reaction and I say, "I'm reacting." I **observe** the reaction as if it's not me. Then what?

ME: So what will that do for you? Why **observe** yourself?

HER: So I can see that I reacted. I can see me *and* the reaction. They are two separate things. Didn't you say that?

ME: I did. If you get the reaction outside yourself, you can see what it's made of, how it works. Have you experienced being the **observer** of your reaction?

HER: I don't do that. I've never done that.

ME: So this will be an interesting experiment, won't it?

HER: I don't even know what to say about that.

She groans and laughs. Such reticence! How tightly we cling to the way we've always done things! I pause while she considers information that doesn't match her established patterns.

ME: You heard his question as criticism of you and decided he's being an asshole because—"How dare he question me about whether I would help him in his old age!" This is one possible interpretation. I'm asking you to think of other possibilities.

HER: Wow. Okay. My brain is feeling weird now. This doesn't make sense and at the same time makes perfect sense.

ME: Don't you love how that works???!!

HER: I don't know. I'll keep you posted!

She's overwhelmed with the question "What else could it be?" Overload during learning is often what it takes to crack our outer cover and reveal the Golden Buddha within—which shines with possibilities! Thought patterns can seem like rocks, they are so solid. But let's see if she is able to hold familiar beliefs less tightly. I'll talk about myself for a while. In the past, taking the spotlight off her loosened things up.

ME: When I am reactive, I figure it's because somewhere in me, I have a button that can be pushed. If I didn't have that button, my husband couldn't push it. He's not doing something to me, but rather I have a button and he just found it for me. What a good thing!

She sits back in her chair. She's relaxing. This is working.

ME: I notice I had a reaction. I see it. I feel it. And I say to myself, "Oh, look! There's my button. What's that button all about?"

HER: Okay, so this problem with him will help me—somewhere, somehow?

ME: It will, if you **observe**. As in, "What a strong reaction I had!" This problem will help you if you get curious and say, "I wonder... Does he know all about my past and what I've done for others in their old age? Maybe not. Maybe he doesn't know me as well as I know myself."

HER: I see what you're saying! How could he possibly know me like I know myself? How could he know what I've done in the past? He hasn't been around me as long as I have.

ME: Yes! You've known him for years, and he's known you, but don't assume he knows all about you. He assumes things, questions you, even accuses you of things that aren't true. He challenges you. Teach him. Teach each other. [I smile and pause briefly.] Maybe he's not against you. He just doesn't know everything about you.

> *She repeats the possibility "Maybe he's not against me. He just doesn't know everything about me" several times. Then her demeanor changes. She becomes tender.*

HER: Sometimes I'm afraid I'll make things worse—he won't like all of me. Heck, I don't even like all of me. I have trouble getting along with myself sometimes. What's he gonna do if he knows ALL about me?

ME: Beautiful. What do you see from this?

HER: I reacted to him because of the way I feel about myself.

ME: You just confirmed that your reaction to him isn't about him. It's about you. Are you beginning to see how this works?

HER: More all the time.

ME: This is one way a partnership can be supportive. A partner can remind us that our reactions to them aren't really about them; they're about us and how we relate. A partner can shine a light on where we don't love ourselves and encourage us to love that place and heal that place. Maybe, if you let him, he could remind you what's to love.

HER: Yeah…

~~~~~

This conversation continues in chapter 21, A Lost Ball and a Bad Game. But this is where she stands for the moment, in contemplation that her reaction to him is actually about her and how she feels about herself. She's been introduced to observation but doesn't quite get it. Yet she's taken steps that are right for her. Her husband has been introduced to observation as well, while in Mouse-in-the-Corner. In chapter 21, he actively participates in the remainder of the session.

Here are some questions we asked in this portion of the conversation:

What if he's not doing what I think he's doing?

- What if he's doing something good?
- What could it be?

What if his questions to me aren't about me?

- If his questions concern him, what could they be?
- Do his questions point to a personal need, to something that's important to him?

What if he's not against me?

- What if he's *for* me? (How does he show that?)
- What if he's looking out for me? (What's the evidence?)
- What if he's looking out for us? (In what ways is he doing that?)

No person can convince you to love yourself. But another person can point the way, like airline workers with flashlights and hand motions for guidance. If your husband has the flashlights, and he guides you toward loving yourself, please don't tell him to bring back the dark. Consider steering in the direction of his signal. Follow his lead.

Any disagreement can highlight the choice to appreciate differences rather than fight about them. One spring day, Eric and I took the humorous route through a conversation that could have gone south in a heartbeat. Either one of us could have become frustrated or offended, but instead, it turned silly. We figured that most anytime was a good time to be lighter about disagreements, or more relaxed as Barbara Jordan suggests: "Think what a better world it would be if we all, the whole world, had cookies and milk about three o'clock every afternoon and then lay down on our blankets for a nap." As the years passed, taking ourselves and our opinions less seriously helped us thrive as a couple.

We were in the midst of a late lunch at home, and the conversation began when Eric asked why vegetables were included on my homemade pizza. He liked only meat and cheese. My reply was that bright colored vegetables make food pretty, which made him laugh. Then we slid into opinionated territory, and I pursued him about his claim to be neutral about mushrooms and pecans. Having discovered a certain delight in being opinionated, I got the giggles. Eric thought it hilarious that we were having a conversation about neutrality while neither of us was being neutral. This kind of humor was right up his alley. So there we were, laughing about being in disagreement.

This sort of play happens when people who care for each other let love lead. Our willingness to be entertained by our strong opinions (rather than upset by them) pulled a whole lot of fun out of practically nothing, and we ended up more in love when it was over. Eric hugged me and said, "Hey, if I'd known that opinions about pizza would cause such a good time, I'd have brought this up long ago."

Three Reminders

Before we leave the subject of how to appreciate differences, note that most arguments are about nothing at all. Nothing. At all. Should there be vegetables on pizza? Should a woman help her husband with a medical test? Should her husband have questioned her? The playful point here is that you can say somebody's wrong (without believing they're wrong), and actually communicate love, respect, and appreciation.

Second, keep in mind that sarcasm is not humor. Being mean-spirited doesn't qualify as funny. To criticize through laughter is a no pass. If there's an edge in your voice, or if the laughter is aimed toward a known wound, that's sleight-of-hand hurtful. So, think and feel before you speak. Be truthful, but be as kind as possible.

Third, the essence of what the two of you believe may not be far apart. Case in point: the husband was looking for reassurance that he would receive needed assistance as he aged, and she was perfectly willing to help him. No problem there. And still they got tripped up on the way to harmony! Eventually she realized, "He's not against me. He just doesn't know everything about me."

In the end, there's nothing to fight about. Instead, discover each other. Be astonished by the beauty of the wide-open landscape of your partner. The biggest secret in the whole world is to have far more fun with your differences. Continue to inquire, "What else could it be?" You may not be on opposite sides, but you may have opposite ways of expressing yourselves.

In this session, she began to observe herself. She took a giant first step in realizing that when she has a reaction, she can separate herself from it in order to see the components and how it works. And because he observed her in the session, he too is obliged to explore "I see my reaction" and "What else could it be?"

~~~~~

Wisdom requires a flexible mind.
—Dan Carlin

20

Core Skill #4: Reflect

TO BREATHE, RECEIVE, and observe summons the next skill: reflect. As we'll use it here, reflection is the custom of finding benefit in an experience, even when benefit isn't immediate or obvious. Reflection can involve sifting the rubble of a difficult time. You may not unearth shiny upsides or bright treasures right away, but if you focus on good stuff, you'll find it. Expect it, and you'll find it faster. The interpretation of a tough situation even slightly in the direction of what's affirmative can position you for future good.

Four years after our marriage fell apart and then got mended, Eric and I decided to move from Los Angeles to the East Coast. We agreed to sell our furniture and set up a $4,000 furniture fund for the new house. Eric sold his car to buy a moving truck and intended to sell the truck for profit once we resettled. My preference was to rent a truck but I left the matter in his hands.

Daughter MacKenzie and I finished packing. She and I drove ahead in my car with pets and essentials, and a week or two later, Eric was scheduled to bring the truck with the rest. My trip with MacKenzie included four animals: three tiny dogs and a cat named Business who was not fond of car trips. Business crawled under the driver's seat and refused to move until we stopped each evening, whereupon he pulled himself out from tight quarters only when offered gourmet tuna. Our three dogs did fine. They thought it was a great adventure.

Not long after Eric got on the road, the truck he'd purchased broke down, and the bill for repairs was almost $4,000. He used the furniture fund to fix the truck. When he called to tell me the news, his words kicked the wind out of me. This was the very situation I had intended to avoid. It would be stressful to set up the new house on a shoestring.

My Practice of the First Four Core Skills

At first I breathed about it. That's all I could do. I breathed a lot. Then I shifted to step two, receive. To make my way toward acceptance of what happened, I stated the facts of the situation aloud as if the facts belonged to another and meant nothing to me. A couple of days later, I was calm enough to claim the facts as mine: "For our cross-country move, we sold most of our furniture and belongings. We agreed on a $4,000 budget to buy used furniture for the new house. Eric sold his car and bought a moving truck. The truck broke down, and the furniture money was used to fix the Isuzu."

My job was to repeat the scenario until I could tell the story like a journalist reporting matter-of-fact data. When the emotion about it faded, my attention turned to acquisition of furniture. If stressful thought patterns turned up again, back to square one I went: name the upsetting thought, breathe, receive, observe, and reflect. To find the good, I sat with the upset to see what it was made of. That softened the impact, and made it possible to look for relief. "This will work out somehow. We'll get the furniture we need, not the way I thought we would, but somehow." Appreciation washed through me each time I noticed and released stress. A useful reflective question was "What if nobody's wrong?" The question helped me move to a freer and more confident place each time.

What began to happen was truly miraculous. Eric made unexpected sales on eBay and handed me cash along with encouragement to head to the consignment store to get the next item. Sometimes he'd surprise me with "Time to go furniture shopping again. How does Thursday afternoon look to you? I'll go with you."

If I had not approached my reflection process with *what if nobody's wrong*, Eric would always be the guy who stole my $4,000 furniture budget. To take my heart off the hook, I took Eric off the hook. Having nobody on the hook allowed me to focus on finding lovely sofas and dressers. And, yes, to get over my initial frame of mind (fear, anger, and blame) required flexibility, faith in myself, and creativity—personal qualities I wished to develop in myself anyway. What an ideal chance to practice.

It's important to know that I did not demand apologies from Eric, or insist that he come up with a new plan for making extra sales. I didn't criticize, punish, or reprimand him. Nor did I withdraw my affection or refuse sex. Not once did he hear, "I told you so" for buying a truck instead of renting one. But when a blameful thought crossed my mind, I sat with the thought until I could find my way to neutral and accept it.

All of my actions centered on my prime interest, which was to make space for solutions. I wanted furniture, and I wanted getting it to feel as easy as a summer breeze floating through an open window. My sincere hope was that taking responsibility for my side of things would allow him to reflect on and handle his side of things, just as he regularly did for me. The knowledge that he was my partner, even when he triggered me, even when he made a "mistake," helped me remember that he was my ally, not my enemy, ever. It was moving to me that when no blame was assigned, Eric stepped up to make sure our new home had everything it needed. My way of being felt both gentle and powerful. It let me relax and feel content. I could go quiet inside. I could love.

Reflection is a powerful tool. Keep it close.

~~~~~

During my short time on earth I have realized
that opportunities are seldom labeled.
—John G. Shedd

21

Conversation: A Lost Ball and a Bad Game

OF ALL THE core skills, reflection probably requires the most emotional agility. There are two sides to reflection. One version is to enhance a positive outcome by savoring it at length, by dwelling on an affirmative end result a little longer. This kind of reflection produces extended happiness.

The challenging version of reflection is the one we'll work with in this chapter. It's the flip side: to examine a negative outcome for its benefits. Finding our way from upset to gratitude obliges us to turn our thinking upside down, to rearrange our take on an incident. Turning a "wrong" into a "right" thrusts our brain into massive reorganization. It grows our ability to express our generous heart and agile mind. (You wanted to do that anyway, didn't you?)

When a couple laughs together, hearts open. The spaciousness and safety of joy invite new questions. We saw this with the couple in chapter 19 whose playful exchange turned serious with the husband's request for health assistance in the future. The wife was offended that he even had to ask whether she would be there for him when he needed her, and she took his queries personally.

Their conversation continues after a discussion about his future health concerns. He's no longer in Mouse-in-the-Corner. We'll explore reflection—how to find benefit in an experience that didn't seem beneficial when it occurred.

~~~~~

HER [to him]: I had no idea that our lighthearted conversation would bring up fears about your future. What I just now heard from you was more information than I knew before. Thank you for sharing all of that.

ME [to both of them]: If you're the one shifting gears in the conversation, you might say, "Okay, we've been joking around, but this brings up a serious question. May I ask it?" To do this, though, you must be aware you've turned a corner; there's something potentially serious you wish to explore.

HER: That would have made all the difference. I'd like to shift gears right now and ask this: what if I have women's intuition? I can tell something's going on and say to him, "You seem a little ill..."

ME: It's good to pay attention to intuition, but perhaps propose a different question.

HER: Like what?

ME: Instead of giving him your interpretation of what you see—"you seem a little ill"—what about first asking for information such as "How are you doing physically? Can you give me an update?"

HER [to him]: So would that be okay?

HIM: Sure.

ME [to him, noticing his slight hesitation]: Is there a different question you'd prefer?

HIM: Actually, I have a comment about the frequency of questions. If we talked about something a week ago, I don't want to be asked again so soon.

HER: Okay.

ME [to her]: Perhaps pose health questions tenderly. Maybe touch him and then ask how he's doing?

HER [to him]: So would you respond well to something like that?

I love that she doesn't take my word for it. She checks with him.

HIM: If you scratched my back, I'd probably answer any question after that! And be prepared for me to reply that I'm fine.

HER [playfully]: Sometimes, though, I want more information. But I've learned that when you're done with the conversation, you're done, and I shouldn't ask you any more questions.

HIM [playing back]: And how do you REALLY feel about that?

HER [laughing hard now]: Yeah, I know. I'm always looking for more details.

Don't you love that their sense of humor has returned? Sweet!

HIM: I think the key here is not being attached to the result.

ME: Would you say more about that?

HIM: I don't want her to project on me what I should say to her. Meaning if she doesn't get what she wants from my response, she's still okay with that.

HER [to him]: I'll be fine. I want you to know that I love to have these conversations lightly whenever possible. I enjoy light and fun. That appeals to me.

ME: Wonderful!

I've made a note to work with him on the courtesy of providing more information. It's a kindness he could offer easily if he reflected on its positive impact. We'll get to it. By the way, there's more on this topic of partners providing information in chapter 24. It's titled "Conversation: Two Angry People Find Love Again."

*Now he launches into demos of what light and fun look and sound like, and she laughs. There's a point in a couple's session where the lid comes off, and that moment is here. Is there a serious topic on the horizon? Are things safe enough to turn a corner? It's chilly outside and we each take a sip of hot tea. We're about to shift gears and **reflect** on a situation that holds quite a bit of gold for them.*

Her Side of the Story

ME: So what's next?

HER: I'd like to talk about what happened on the golf course a few days ago. My ball disappeared behind a tree, and I tried to describe to him where the ball was so he could get it. I pointed to the tree.

HIM: To the group of trees…

HER: Whatever way I explain it, it will be wrong, even now in this session with you, Terri. My description won't be specific enough. It won't be accurate. We were on the eighteenth hole, and he had not had a good round.

HIM: That's for sure.

HER: And I was playing pretty well. Our friend was also playing well.

HIM: Which totally pissed me off.

HER: So I made a concerted effort to stay on my game while being sympathetic to his circumstances. I kept my mouth shut about his string of bad shots. I didn't say, "Gee, I'm sorry you're having a terrible round." Everybody has their own game, their own mindset. On the golf course, my philosophy is that it's better to keep most thoughts to yourself. Less talk is better.

Anyway, I directed him to my lost ball, but not the way he preferred. I kept wondering, "Gosh, how can I describe the ball location so he understands me???" He got angry! There was no way to tell him exactly how to get my ball. It wasn't the third tree to the left or anything simple like that. I pointed and said, "It's over that way, on that path, on that bank." He snarled back, "Which bank?" Nothing I said worked. He was not happy. I was not happy. Nobody was happy.

To solve things, I made my way to the ball. Then I took a deep **breath** to bring myself into the present moment. I needed to hit it just right to get it back on the fairway and make it playable, which I knew would be a challenge for me. I hit it well, and he said, "Good shot." I was concentrating on the path of the shot in order to avoid the trouble of another ball search if it went off course. Before I could acknowledge his compliment, he barked, "You're welcome." My silent response was, "GAWD. This is just the way it is, isn't it?"

It was tough. We talked about it when we got home, and he apologized. He said he was having a terrible round, and he was sorry. He owned it. I wish we could recover sooner, though, and not spend so many hours upset. That's what I want.

His Side of the Story

ME [to her]: Thank you for that story. Let's see what we can do about your request.

ME [to him]: Will you give me your version of this ball-in-the-trees story?

HIM: I was driving the cart, and first of all, her statement about how nothing she said would have gotten me to the ball is absolutely not true. More meat on the bones, more detail about which tree would have been helpful. I take exception to her comment that nothing would have worked. Also, my upset near the end of the golf game was a cumulative thing. I was frustrated—on to the next shot, but still in my head about the previous one. Forgive me, what was your question again?

ME: I want to hear your version of the lost ball story.

HIM: Right. So what I heard was, "It's by the tree!" I could have said to her, "Give me more information because that's not enough to go on."

ME: She may or may not have been able to give you details that would satisfy you. She had a sense of where the ball was. She had a feeling about where it was. But it's not always easy to describe a sense or feeling of location because, from personal experience, I can tell you it tends to move and change as you get closer to the ball. When she turns on her "find it" radar, she's sensing where it is as she closes in on it. She finds a lost ball differently than you do.

With this, she looks up. She is clearly touched by this description.

His Work

ME: One way to stay out of the weeds emotionally is to get curious instead of angry. Specifically, be curious about how to keep your love for each other intact while you solve the problem at hand. How might you do that? Can you give me some ideas?

HIM: I'm not sure what you're getting at.

ME: I'm asking you to tell me how you might be loving toward her even though you're upset about your game.

HIM: I'm not sure I can do that.

ME: True. And—there's your work.

> *We pause here. He needs time to consider this idea. He was upset with his performance on the course, and placed the burden of betterment on her—if she could just explain the location of the ball, he could find it and his day would improve!*
>
> *The irony here is not lost on you, I'm sure. You've seen that when she asks for information ("how are you feeling"), he refuses to elaborate. When he asks for information from her ("tell me how to get to your ball"), he expects to get it and that her words will give him a win.*
>
> *Now back to his work: find a way to remain loving toward her even when he's upset.*

ME: If you're mad on the golf course, who are you upset with?

HIM: Well, myself, I suppose. My game was off. Also, I was driving the cart, so that was an added dynamic. Okay, I will try "kinder and gentler." I think my day had affected me negatively, and I was not at my best.

ME: But you're not always at your best. Then what?

HIM: Point taken.

ME: I'll repeat my comment. But you're not always at your best. Then what?

> *She's listening intently. My attention is focused on him, but we're not in Mouse-in-the-Corner. She could jump in at any time. Let's see if he's up for some new alternatives.*

ME: Observe yourself on this sunny golf day with friends. The inquiry is, why get careless about your connection with her because your game is in the toilet?

He listens intently and nods. But so far he's not stepping up to the plate. She's relaxing. I'm smiling.

ME: Make any problem a joint project: "Won't it be fun when we figure out where this ball is? I bet we can do this." Be like kids on a playground.

They are both notably calm. I wonder if past scenes from their partnership have overtaken their awareness. Perhaps pages of their relationship history are flipping through their minds. She ventures back into the conversation.

HER: What you're saying makes sense. It's just that we don't do that at all, not even close. I bet this is his thought, too, how we don't do this at all. [He nods.]

With this statement, she returns to silence. It's efficient to give ourselves time and space during a change moment. Where will she take this? When she's ready, she begins to walk herself through a new possibility.

Her New Story

HER: He could say to me, "Maybe you can't tell me where it is," and I could say, "Well, I know it's on this bank where I'm pointing."

The tone of her voice is exploratory as she takes small steps that rewrite the part of the conversation where they had trouble.

HER: I could say to him, "If you'll just take the cart in the direction of my finger, we will get in the vicinity of my ball, and I'll tell you when to stop."

He has stepped out of the conversation for now. He has good reasons, I'm sure, and he'll reenter when he's ready. For now I take his cue and talk with her.

ME [to her]: What would you like to do differently next time?

HER: I wish I had directed him better, but his anger threw me.

ME: Is there a way you can make his emotion less significant in your mind?

HER: An angry man in my presence is hard for me.

ME: When both of you are reactive what can you do?

HER: One of us has to change something!

ME: Which one of you was in the best shape at that moment? Who had the ability to pull things out of the nosedive?

HER: Probably me.

ME: Then perhaps nominate yourself to change something?

HER: Sometimes I'm good at that and sometimes not.

ME: True.

HER: I think I can learn to let him do what he needs to do and stay out of it.

HIM [jumps back in]: Unless it becomes personal. When it's about you, it's harder for you.

> *Notice that he stepped back in, not to offer a solution or take responsibility but rather to point to her "problem." This is valuable information about his habits, and where he stands.*

HER [answering him]: Yep. [She turns to me.] But when we drive, he yells with rage at other drivers which is scary, too. I don't do well when he's angry or loud.

HIM [snapping to attention and interrupting her]: Oh, that's an exaggeration! Rage is a strong word. I wasn't raging.

> *I'm sure you noticed what just happened. Is he **receiving** her? No. He's defending himself. He has demonstrated exactly how he interacts with her at home. Again, helpful information.*

HER [throwing up both arms]: Okay! So here's another place we argue! I take things personally. He takes things literally.

ME: How can this knowledge help you?

Maybe I Should Hold Myself Back

HER: This is really tough for me. I make a statement, and then it seems I have to reel it back in, because it causes trouble with him.

ME: You enjoy using words more loosely than literally, yes? It's a little bit fun and dramatic to call it rage, right?

> *This question causes her to twinkle with laughter. Her beauty flows out of her.*

HER: Oh yeah! It is! It's way fun for me! [She turns more serious.] But not for him. So what should I do? Call it upset instead of rage?

> *This "shall I change to accommodate my partner" idea comes up fairly often in sessions. One partner attempts to keep the peace, usually at the cost of their self-expression and happiness.*

ME: What would it be like for you to begin to adjust your descriptive choices just for him?

HER: I don't know. I think I'd hold back around him, as if something's wrong with me, as if I have to fix how I say things.

ME: How might that affect you over time?

HER: I'd have to go play with others if how I express myself isn't welcome here. Over time, I think we might grow apart.

ME: Is that the direction you want to go? Apart?

HER: No.

ME: What could you do instead?

HER: Well, I could be myself and let him deal with it.

ME: How do you think that might go?

HER: I'd need to teach him about me, like you said before.

ME: You would. Are there bonuses to teaching him about you?

HER: I'm sure I'd learn about myself, too. I wonder if we could do that together. I'd like that.

ME: What a beautiful project! Teach him about you. Learn about him. Learn about you. If you give him your natural self, both of you can figure out how to deal with true-you.

> *She nods, smiles big. She's all lit up again. She is exploring how she might have it both ways—keep peace and be herself. Brilliant.*

ME: When you express in your dramatic manner, maybe he'll object. Maybe he'll correct you. If you don't take his response personally, that leaves him with his own reaction, and it might help him work out his side of things. Let him do that. Let this be an equal opportunity.

When he tells you that rage is the wrong word, enjoy him. Learn about him. When he asks you to play his way, which is to be specific and defined, try it. Make it a game and ask for feedback. "Okay, let me see if I can do it. Here I go…" How does life work from his point of view? And then teach him about your playful ways. "Oh, there I go again! Whatever will we do with my dramatic side?" Encourage him to play with your love of exaggeration and drama. Offer him true-you, so he can learn about—and appreciate—true-you.

You're not on opposite sides. But we could say you have opposite ways of expressing. Rather than alter your style, why not enjoy your differences? Differences are love puddles. Go ahead, step in them. Get wet.

They both smile.

ME: Make each other right, too. I mean, why not? Don't we love validation?

HER: Well, he doesn't tell me I'm right…

> *There is competition between the two of them about being right. In past sessions we've spoken of this, and we speak briefly about it now. Clearly, there's more to do on the subject. I make a note.*

HIM: I do think men are geared toward the literal, and my training is in that direction as well. I believe that accurate words are critical to getting a point across. If words are improper or ineffective, then the intended communication can get distorted and cause unintended consequences. In one of my jobs, the belief was that miscommunication happens because we don't possess a command of the language. There were dictionaries in every room. All of this is to say I did not rage in the car. Because if we looked it up, we would find that rage is not accurate. My actions wouldn't fit the definition.

Where Does His Love Go?

ME: We understand. But you're missing the point.

He is waiting for me to say more here, but I am quiet. Asking questions seems to be a lost art with him. He could use some help with being curious instead of defensive, and asking instead of stating. I'll speak in a way that hopefully invites questions from him. We'll see how this goes.

HIM: I'm not sure I understand what you intend here.

He didn't ask a question. I'll give it another shot.

ME: I'm asking how you might prioritize a loving response.

HIM: I don't see where you're going.

I speak with both of them about the value of asking questions.

ME: My point is this: when nailing a golf shot trumps all else, where does your love go? When you miss a shot, where is your self-approval then? And where is your approval and support of your wife?

HIM: Still not following you. Oh, right, I should ask a question. Well, I'm not sure where my approval of her is when I'm upset.

He laughs a little, presumably in recognition that he still didn't ask a question. This new habit of inquiry may take some time to adopt. I'll continue my support of this.

ME: My dear man, you've got a *woman* in front of you, not a business problem, or a room full of dictionaries. A goddess stands before you. A brilliant, beautiful, sexual, sensual, joyful creature. A complete mystery. You have the kind of woman J. D. Salinger talked about when he said, "She wasn't doing a thing that I could see, except standing there, leaning on the balcony railing, holding the universe together." You might want to investigate whether your propensity to define separates you from her. [I smile at him and use a dramatic arm sweep.] In the bedroom, perhaps toss the darn dictionary...

HIM: Oh. Well.

> *He's working with new ideas, but our time is up. In the future, I'll ask more about his take on women, partnership, and love. And I'll take advantage of his love of definitions. But for now I'm going to seize the quick route out of this productive discussion.*

ME [to him]: If you toss the dictionary out of the bedroom, you would—for sure—have better sex with your beautiful wife.

HIM: Oh! Well, I'm all for that!

HER: Me too. Whatever we're up to, you would tell us to get more curious. Ask more questions, teach each other. Time in the bedroom is way more fun without dictionaries.

~~~~~

Needless to say, many subjects were raised during this session, but we were at the maximum for one sit-down. She embraced her fair share of challenges in this session, but he has some catch-up to do. Were some topics still unfolding? Certainly. Will they continue to reveal themselves in coming sessions? No doubt. Do they have clear assignments? Yes, and we recapped those before they left.

When two people both want to be right, the relationship is competitive. Competition in sports works fine. Competition in an intimate relationship, however, is a foul. Blow the whistle if you prefer intimacy and connection with each other. Love is not basketball.

This was a beginning lesson on reflection. Their golf day set them up with adverse outcomes, and we looked for value in them. We asked questions.

- Was his grumpy mood more important than his love for her and his kindness toward her?
- How can she remain centered when he's angry?

- How can they feel free to be themselves yet enjoy their differences?
- What would it take to make it through the day without getting tripped up by each other?
- And what about dictionaries versus great sex?

So much to explore! Reflecting on our differences encourages us to appreciate the diversity and strength they offer. The positive ripple effect is that by working out personal differences, there is a greater chance of improving relationships on the local, national, or worldwide level as well. We can accomplish globally only what we understand personally.

To make strides in your local government or your community, there is something you can do. Turn your attention to your small corner of existence, and do your personal, powerful work inside you: breathe, receive, observe, and reflect. Peace in you, harmony with your partner and with your family, and collaboration in the world—all of these begin with your conscious breath.

~~~~~

> How is it they live in such harmony the
> billions of stars—when most men
> can barely go a minute without declaring war in
> their minds about someone they know.
> —Thomas Aquinas

22

Core Skill #5: Rehearse

THIS IS A core skill with two aspects. Rehearsal can be intentional, for instance to practice the delivery of a speech. Or for another example, we can deliberately choose to respond with patience when our child launches into a predictable breakdown—teach ourselves to breathe and take a pause before we blurt something we'll regret later. We do our best, make adjustments, and then do it over again. This type of rehearsal reinforces our positive intention, and with consistent repetition, our new way of being takes hold.

However, rehearsal can also be unintentional or automatic. Recall the earlier quote from Dr. Joe Dispenza that describes how programmed we are by age thirty-five. We've memorized a set of behaviors and thoughts that have become our identity and personality. Some of our patterns, established through countless unintentional rehearsals, are to our advantage, such as using humor or light-heartedness to brush off a failed attempt. However, rehearsal of automatic negative reactions such as anger, critical pushback, or over-consumption of food and drink in the face of disagreement or stress, does us no favors.

What Are We Rehearsing in Partnerships?

In a partnership—ideally—what exactly are we rehearsing? We are practicing our capacity to love. To be born is to be handed the challenge. There's no out. And yes, the practice of love (being true-you) takes a lifetime.

In our daily love practice, we have two choices: suffer or be free. Freedom sounds like a good choice, right? We think being free means we can do whatever we choose. But truly, freedom is different from that. Freedom requires the use of the core skill of receiving: surrender to what is said, felt, done. All the rest is resistance, which causes suffering. Even the attempt to protect ourselves from pain causes suffering. Avoidance of suffering causes suffering. To be free, let love be your teacher. Your heart will break. Let it. The only way a heart can break is open. Each time your heart breaks, old defenses (not-you) drop away. A broken-open heart is real and available. It's true-you.

The first four core skills (breathe, receive, observe, reflect) light the path to true-us. This fifth skill—rehearse—supports and reinforces our discoveries. An average day's events provide countless opportunities to find and practice who we are. The use of core skills is transferable across all aspects of life. The practice of the core skills as you play tennis (receive or observe, for instance) is helpful later in a financial conversation with your spouse, by consciously connecting the two (transfer skills from the tennis court to finances). Bravery you summoned for your community theater audition can be harnessed to speak truth to your mate over dinner. Your innovative leadership during a company meeting can benefit those same creative muscles in your intimate partnership.

To test how intentional rehearsal works, learn a new activity that pushes you a bit. A half day at a zip line course might do the trick. A dance class requiring more coordination than you're accustomed to would suffice. Even driving a new route to a familiar destination without Google Maps on the dashboard could be enough of a challenge for some of us.

Let's say you decide to take a leap. You sign up for a group voice class, followed by a performance. Singing is an excellent choice, because it is intensely personal. It reveals secret and unspoken opinions we hold about ourselves. It exposes what we believe others think of us, as well as how much stock we place in their opinions. The act of singing illuminates emotional stresses at play in our intimate relationships, too, because what we discover about ourselves as we sing holds true at home as well.

The brilliance of taking a leap to learn something new is that it unlocks the "you" you're automatically rehearsing each day. That "you" shows up front and center. This is enormously helpful. When core skills—breathe, receive, observe, and reflect—are used to work with what shows up, it makes what was invisible visible, and what was unconscious conscious. When you unlock your established patterns, you'll notice what risks you tend to avoid, or how fear of rejection or judgment keeps you quiet. Bringing ourselves and our habits into the light is an act of love. In the light, it's easier to see what to keep and what to let go of, what's true-you and what's not-you. In the light, love shows up. It shines brighter.

My Personal Experience

Being a voice student trained me to learn in front of others. This was not something I enjoyed at first, but gradually my fear decreased and my defenses lowered. The level of my embarrassment also diminished. Public mistakes became less of a big deal with each class or singing performance. The process took quite a few years.

There were parallels between voice class and my relationship with Eric. Fear of being vulnerable showed up in class (to volunteer to sing first or sing when I felt unprepared). This same self-protection showed up with Eric when I felt hesitant to confess something or when it was difficult to expose myself to his input. Singing for others helped me see the ways I protected myself. When I observed my learned habits, they became visible. With light on them, I could make a conscious choice to unlearn an old habit—stop rehearsing protection in my relationship with Eric—and choose to start rehearsing curiosity and an open heart.

Much later, following my stint as a student singer and performer, in addition to my work as a relationship coach, I co-taught a group voice class for eight to ten singers. Students were amazed how quickly their resident opinions and beliefs surfaced. It was practically impossible to keep them hidden. We encouraged students to make friends with whatever came up, because it would help them to sing freely, but would also assist them in life. We sing the way we live.

Safety

Because emotional discovery in public can feel unsettling, we designed a safe learning environment. When a singer completed a solo, we asked two things.

1. What did you do well?
2. What do you want help with?

Almost without exception, singers found it difficult to state what they did well. Instead, they would stall or fidget. They'd talk about something else. "What did you do well?" brings powerful self-love questions into the light:

> "What if other people don't think I did well and I think I did?"

> "My song wasn't that good. Why give myself credit for mediocrity?"

> "It feels indulgent to pat myself on the back. Wouldn't it be more productive to use my time to fix what I did wrong instead?"

Can you imagine how these same emotional defaults affect dating? Marriage? Having children? Support or approval of a mate? It's time for some reassuring science. Dr. Rick Hanson, psychologist and researcher, states that human survival is based on being wired to pay attention to the one thing that could endanger our life—an enemy approaching, a stick thrown, a falling rock. This is known as negative bias. We underplay ten good things that happened: I found food. The sun is shining. I'm strong. I run fast. My vision is excellent. Edible plants cover this hillside. Isn't this land beautiful? There's a rabbit I can eat. I have shelter. I'm safe.

Negative bias is present when learning something new, whether it's how to sing or how to initiate a conversation with your mate about a difficult subject. Rather than stamp out or turn away from negative bias, evolve it. Recognize it, give a nod of inclusion, and then deliberately search for a favorable focus. Our survival intelligence doesn't naturally scan for the best aspects of our vocal performance, or highlight the five top features of how our mate cleans a bathroom. That's why we requested that our students pay deliberate attention to what they did well. We encouraged them to train their brains to look for good stuff. And hooray! We can curb our automatic rehearsal of negative bias. Our brains are teachable.

Self-Criticism

One benefit of singing for others is that we become aware of what muzzles our expression. If self-criticism holds you back as you sing for an audience, it holds you back in your partnership, too. Take the time to take a look.

Singers sometimes say (or secretly think), "Ugh. I don't like how I sang that high note." To cringe about how we sound holds pretty harsh judgment. But if you shine a light on self-criticism and consider its messages—truly receive them—you can see what you've been rehearsing, and make a decision whether to continue. You might make a choice to rehearse self-expression instead. When criticism's revealing work is done, fear steps back and love moves in.

Not Good Enough

Apology comes up when a singer jokingly warns listeners through words and physical cues that a song they're about to perform won't be good, or good enough, or as good as it should be, which is to say, "I'm sorry you must hear me." Our apology shows itself in lack of vigor and in our posture, too. If we're an apologetic parent, of course we teach apology to our children—how could we not? Backpedaling about a solo is a little like breaking up with someone before they break up with you. Or it's like saying, "I'm sorry to bother you, but..." To dread an important conversation because we're concerned that it won't go well is often apology in advance.

Voice class helped singers move the feeling of "less than" from hidden to visible, where we could observe and work with our responses in safe ways as a group. We discussed where apology shows up with our mate or with a supervisor at work. We spoke about how appreciation of our sound might help us rehearse appreciation in other areas of our life.

Comparison

Danish philosopher Søren Kierkegaard said, "Comparison is the most dangerous acquaintance love can make." In class we spoke about how awful it feels to compare ourselves to another singer. We addressed this better-than, worse-than seesaw so that singers could recognize it and breathe about it—sing through it. We observed that it's common to think "She's so much better than I am. She doesn't make vocal mistakes where I would."

Similarly, relationship consulting clients have shared their thoughts with me about comparison, that surely others have easier mates, fewer upsets, and more fun in the bedroom. Comparison is never a win-win. Somebody loses, and it's usually us. Theodore Roosevelt called comparison "the thief of joy." When comparison comes up in singing (or another learning experience you choose), it's possible to spot where else in your life it lives. Then, you can soften your approach. Rather than compare yourself to others, notice what unique qualities and skills you bring to the mix and put your attention there. With your welcome light on them, the qualities that shine as "the best of you" will grow. And each time you interrupt and call off your habit of comparison, you get better at keeping it from the driver's seat. You are finding and practicing true-you using the power of rehearsing.

Being All-In

Voice is powerful. To sing as true-us requires every muscle, every emotion, and all of our senses. If you sing, even in your own living room, you can break the habit of allowing negativity to call the shots. Musical genius Bobby McFerrin suggests improvisational singing for ten minutes a day as an exercise for singers, but it works for anyone who wishes to release self-judgment or restraint. Wild singing (as if no one's listening) is by nature an expression of love 'cause we're all-in.

According to Dr. Rick Hanson, one practice is especially helpful to evolve our tendency to focus on what's wrong:

> Several times a day, take in the good by really savoring a positive experience for 10–20 seconds or more. [The second chapter of *Just One Thing* is about this.] Over time, much as repeated negative experiences make the brain more sensitive to them, I believe that repeatedly savoring positive experiences can train your brain to internalize them increasingly rapidly—in effect, making your brain like Velcro for the positive and Teflon for the negative.[30]

As you learn a new skill, use it to discover dark corners, yes, but also to find your bright competencies. Then rehearse them. Celebrate and share them! Taking appropriate risks helps you realize so much about yourself and contributes directly to the depth and quality of your daily existence on this beautiful planet. Go ahead. Kick off your shoes. Tackle something new, and see what you learn about true-you!

~~~~~

> Be who you were created to be,
> and you will set the world on fire.
> —Saint Catherine of Sienna

Anger
can
be
a
sign
of
positive
progress.

23

The Upside of Anger

SOON YOU'LL HAVE the privilege of listening in on a couple's conversation that brings together all five core skills. The primary emotion present in this spirited conversation is anger. We often think of anger as something to be controlled or at least shunted. However, if it is seen as a benevolent messenger, then it serves us, as this couple discovers.

Have you observed that fierce anger feels like an internal volcano rising? The body provides plenty of fuel to get our heated reaction up and out! Adrenaline and cortisol increase heart rate and breathing, and we get a shot of energy. If we've been tired or down in the dumps, having a personal explosion can be a sign of life. Though chronic wrath is not healthy, anger does have benefits if we listen: What's got our attention? What's important to us? What do we need? In a mentally healthy person, anger is not something to squelch. It is not an enemy. Instead, pay attention. Observe yourself. Give a passionate speech in your living room about what's wrong, and listen as you speak, or record it for later playback. A clear message may jump out at you. Anger is bursting with eventual good news.

Think of anger as one floor of a multistory tower of emotions. The bottom floors are despair, powerlessness, fear, and depression. The next floors up are landings for another layer of quiet (often private) emotions: guilt, unworthiness, and insecurity. Outrage is above that, and because outrage has life energy, an unexpected burst of it pulls us up from bottom-floor despair through those first dark, disempowering emotions—fast! A healthy dose of indignation can even propel us toward hope.

Of course, upset can prove difficult for those around you. They may prefer the quiet and civil version of you. For them, your temper is inconvenient, and besides, you're a handful—loud, out of control, unpredictable. But if you resist the expression of ferocious feelings, those feelings hold you hostage. They sap your energy. You might as well let them up and out. Being exasperated and having a good yell about it can be life-affirming. As with other emotions, anger is your partner, and asks for your hand. Together, hear its message and head toward honest-to-god you.

Let's say you lost yourself in a relationship. Now you want your strength and life force back. Imagine being on the elevator of the aforementioned emotional tower. Where did you leave your nerve, your bravery, your backbone? You try the first few floors. No power there. Then the door opens on the floor labeled I'm-Angry-as-Hell-and-I'm-Not-Gonna-Take-It-Anymore. This has potential! Look around. Receive what's there. Take it in. Here, find conversations: the recent one with your difficult landlord, yesterday's encounter with imperious Aunt Margie, and the self-respect you left behind in both cases. Notice the history of your recent intimate relationship spilled in front of you, too, along with abandoned grit, moxie, and fearlessness!

As soon as you find the energy from those pieces of self-respect and strength, scoop it into your arms, return to the elevator, and push the up button toward contentment, hopefulness, optimism, enthusiasm, and appreciation. Through a ceremony, bring the recouped energy home to your heart, lungs, and voice. Dance the energy back in, or imagine it rejoining you during meditation, for instance. You'll notice an immediate difference in the way you feel as the energy returns to circulation. And by the way, that's a lot of energy!

When you explore intense displeasure, do your best to create the fewest possible casualties. Be awake, not sloppy, with your flare ups (don't aim them at innocent people). If you notice you're shoveling annoyance all over others, seek assistance from someone who sees the good in you. Find a flexible type who won't take sides and knows the value of where you stand and where you're headed. Talk with them.

Next, consider two types of anger.

Conscious Anger

I'm conscious of heat rising within me. I'm mad as a wet hen, but I'm 100 percent aware that I'm triggered. My awareness allows me to step outside the emotion to observe the one who's angry (me).

It's my truth that nobody did anything to me. Nobody *made* me upset. Instead, I'm responsible; it's my emotional trigger. No one else is the cause of this reaction of mine and no other person will pay. There will be no civilian casualties.

My heated state isn't for the purpose of blame, shame, control, or punishment. Rather, blowing my top is an occasion to listen to my words and address an issue. If I'm reacting to injustice, for instance, I might aim my attention and energy toward community change that matters most to me.

Unconscious Anger

I've fallen into the bubbling-rage-cauldron and can't separate myself from my strong emotion. I am the anger, and the anger is me. I act it out. I go wherever my outrage sends me.

My stance is: I'm foaming at the mouth—hey, anyone would be! This is not my fault. My upset is justified. This troubling issue is all over me, and I will get it all over you, too. I can't help myself. Anger is not my partner, and it teaches me nothing, because I'm not listening.

It's good to be familiar with these two distinct kinds of anger and to comprehend that there are choices. If being ticked off gets the best of you often, here are four approaches from Wayne Sotile, PhD, author of *Thriving with Heart Disease*.[31]

- Give yourself an out by saying, "If I'm still angry about this tomorrow, I'll deal with it then. But for now I'm just going to cool off."
- Remind yourself that nothing is accomplished by blaming other people, even if they are responsible for the problem. Try another angle.
- Ask yourself: will this matter five years from now? (Five hours? Five minutes?)
- Realize that acting angry is not the same as showing that you care.

Though anger can be difficult, it's more satisfying than feeling powerless, depressed, or fearful. An athlete shared details of a ski accident early in his career that resulted in a botched surgery, a life-threatening infection, and almost a year of recovery time away from his beloved mountains. He was upset with the surgeons, nurses, and even his own family. Underneath it all, he felt fearful. Would he ever ski again?

For him, anger was uncomfortable, but on the positive side, it gave him the energy to face his challenge. When he stood up for himself, medical personnel were suddenly required to answer questions and make adjustments. And yes, he skied again, for many successful years. He worked his way from being enveloped by agitation and run by it back to his life passion and to the mountains he loved.

The next couple's conversation offers examples of both conscious and unconscious anger. Hang on to your hat; this session is full of spunk and spice. You'll feel their waves of exasperation as they travel the winding road back to adoration and appreciation. They finally get there, and you'll love how it ends.

~~~~~

> If we wish to express anger fully, the first step is to divorce
> the other person from any responsibility for our anger.
> —Marshall B. Rosenberg

Ideally,
anger
is
a short
stop,
a
way
station.

24

Conversation: Two Angry People Find Love Again, Part 1

A COUPLE WALKS into my office upset. They've been together for two years and are struggling with a recent event. I've worked with both of them prior to today as individuals and also as a couple. They are here because she is afraid and confused. She has lost her safe, loving connection with her partner. She isn't sure what's hers to shift and what's his. His fiery outbursts have thrown her off-center. When he gets angry, she loses her confidence, ease, and the desire to be with him. She describes his behavior this way: "One day he's wet spaghetti, and another day, a bomb."

He, too, knows something needs to change but has no clear grasp on how to make things better. He's confused about why he gets unnerved. He doesn't like the way his temper shows up around the woman he loves and is actively looking for assistance.

Both want to feel connected and in love again. They adore each other and are committed to the relationship, even with an added challenge ahead. Soon he'll move out of state, and at least for a time, they will endure a long-distance relationship. For now, though, something shook their love-applecart, and it sent bruised apples bouncing. They enter my office solemnly, no eye contact with each other and barely with me. They settle into chairs quietly and each takes a drink of water.

This conversation is a long one, and it is a goldmine. Not only is it about anger, but it's a review of our Survival Selves and the five core skills. The conversation is divided into three parts. Take your time and digest the material in each section to allow key lessons to settle before moving on. References to the five core skills are in bold font.

~~~~~

ME: How may I be of assistance?

HIM: After my last session with you, Terri, things from the past came up that took me by surprise. This is our last week together [he gestures to his girlfriend] before I leave for a while. But I don't see a way around asking her for time to work through some things that surfaced. I needed time to think, and she didn't give it to me. I got pissed. This is what I do. I get upset when things don't go my way. Being disagreeable has created issues in past relationships and again in this one. This anger thing doesn't work. It confines me. I need to know what else I've got—other than anger.

ME [to him]: Well, let me first say thank you for a brilliant question: what else do I have besides anger? What a great place to begin.

> *He settles into his chair, leans back. She takes a deep breath and looks at her lap.*

ME [to both of them]: First, you are where you are. Relax as much as you can. We'll work this out today. Together, we can do this.

ME [to her; she is now in tears]: So, my dear, tell me about you.

HER: Something came out of left field. It seemed like things were fine with us. Then he came home Tuesday, and he's "gone." Absent! Nobody home! He leaves soon for a month. I was given no particulars, just left out in the cold. His distance and reserve lead me to believe he's leaving the relationship.

> *She's turned toward me, head cocked, completely aghast about this possibility.*

HER: I mean, what the heck is going on? Is this an effort to let me down gently? Will he just fade into the horizon, ride off into the sunset, or what? And on top of all my fear, I was berated for feeling that way!

ME: Tell me about his request to take some time, go inside, and figure out a few things about his past.

HER [yells]: HE DIDN'T MAKE A REQUEST!!! He said, "I'M WORKING WITH SOME THINGS, AND I JUST NEED TO BE INSIDE." [She pauses, backs off, self-adjusts.] Okay. So…he did make a request.

But in an instant she's furious again and stands up to yell— and she's got volume! She punctuates her message, fists to thighs, and dips five times for emphasis.

HER: BUT. WHAT. DOES. THAT. MEAN???

She sits down but continues with emphatic gestures. She's rockin'-rollin' angry.

HER: Does it mean we don't talk to each other? We don't touch? We haven't touched each other in three days! Are we to act like strangers now because he needs to THINK about his freaking past? We've been doing well, and suddenly he's in the kitchen with me, and we're strangers?!? Give me a break! Will somebody just tell me what's going on? If I know what's the matter, I can deal with it.

Her Turn

ME [taking a deep breath, I turn to him]: I'll work with her. Time for Mouse-in-the-Corner, okay?

*He nods his approval. We've done Mouse-in-the-Corner before, so he knows he'll **observe**, quiet as a mouse.*

ME [to her]: Are you also okay with Mouse-in-the-Corner? [She nods.] What did we hear from this upset person?

HER [flipping her right hand in the air]: I don't f-ing know.

> *She takes a long pause here. To answer my question, she'll need to shift gears. I'm asking her to step out of her bubbling pot of unconscious anger long enough to* **observe** *what she does or says, which has been the emphasis in our recent sessions. Once calm, she answers.*

HER: She feels alone? Scared? Confused?

ME: Good. Yes. All of that.

> *We'll go slow here and be present to her strong emotion in order to meet it and get to know what drives it.*

ME: What else are we getting? Tell me more.

HER: She fumes. She's full of fire.

ME: About what?

HER: About change.

ME: How does she deal with change?

HER: Not well. Especially when it comes out of nowhere.

ME: Maybe it didn't come out of nowhere.

HER [leaping out of her chair and yelling at full volume]: IT DID COME OUT OF NOWHERE! He left and talked to you! He came back a different person! What the hell! It came out of damn nowhere!!!!

*I pause for another deep **breath**. Yes, I'm practicing the core skills. Blame is pouring out of her—better out than in. My job is to **receive** her. As best I can, I'll step into her shoes to understand what's there for her.*

ME: I get the sense you may have decided, "Terri's wrong. He's wrong. Heck, maybe the two of us ganged up on you."

HER: Yes! EXACTLY!

ME: Okay...let's get this idea about who's wrong and why loosened up a bit. 'Cause right now I can hardly breathe.

HER: WELL, THAT MAKES TWO OF US.

ME: Look. I know you. I see you. I love you. Thank you for everything you've expressed. Can we listen to the messages from this angry woman and learn from her words? Would that work for you?

*She nods and tears stream down her face. Again, I'm asking her to **observe**. I'll get things started and speak about her as if we're watching her.*

ME: This angry woman is having difficulty with a recent change. Her boyfriend went to see Terri, and after the session, he requested time to disappear into an inner process. When this change occurred, what did she say or do?

HER: She said he was at fault for leaving her out in the cold.

ME: Yes. She thought, "He's left me with no details, no clues about what this means. Who knows the status of our relationship!"

HER: She's deserted and in stress.

ME: How does this leave her?

HER: She's powerless, a victim.

ME: And does that work for her?

HER: It doesn't work. At all.

ME: Then she does what?

HER: She yells. But it doesn't really get rid of her fear. She's still terrified.

ME: Shall we investigate how the core skills can help you? [She nods.] Go ahead and start us off.

HER: To begin, **breathe**. Calm myself. Let my inner wisewoman step up. Then **receive**. Take in what happened. Step back to **observe**. If I **reflect**, I'll see how the situation is here to help me. I know it's for my benefit, even though I don't see how yet.

ME: You'll get there as you move from being angry toward being curious.

HER: What difference would it make if I were more curious?

ME: If you step back and say, "Look what showed up in my world. I'm doing my best with this..."

HER [interrupting]: I know that.

ME: How so? Can you tell me more?

She leans forward and roars.

HER: I've been through SO MUCH G-DAMN F-ING GRATITUDE about my life lately. My anxiety level is LOW compared to what it used to be. I don't wake up with fear anymore. I don't have a damn income right now, and I'm FINE.

She becomes radiant with the statement about her income. Her face changes, her posture, her tone of voice. Her mood lightens.

HER: I have no idea what I'm going to do yet, and I'm at peace with it. I've surrendered!

ME [after a pause for the impact of her words]: You became radiant just now as you described it.

HER: Yes, I felt that.

> *We take time to anchor reasons for her radiance. We talk about similar situations from her past in which she felt confident even in uncertain circumstances.*

ME: Can the surrender you've experienced in the past inform you now?

HER: Hmmm. I could translate what I already know to this new situation.

> *She ponders this, and then her demeanor shifts. Suddenly she drips with sarcasm. She walks a fine line here, the one where you get reckless on purpose in order to find emotions shoved under the rug. What she's about to do is a good thing.*

HER [with heavy sarcasm]: So I'd say,

> "He leaves for a month on Monday. I'm fine."
> "He behaves like an asshole. I'm fine."
> "He has distanced himself from me. I'm fine."

ME: You could say any of those things. What else might you say?

HER: I could say that I'm upset, and I don't understand any of this right now. But I know I'll understand it more as I go.

> *It's suddenly clear she could use a break.*

ME: Why don't you rest for a while? Just take it easy for a bit, and I'll work with him.

HER: Thank you. I'd love that.

> *She sits back, crosses her legs in a yoga pose on the chair, takes a long drink of water. I turn to him. Mouse-in-the-Corner is over for him, and now she's the **observer**. This is how sessions with couples ebb and flow. I work with one person until there's a shift in energy.*

His Turn

HIM: I just wanted some trust. I thought, "I can't rescue you. I'm dealing with my own crap, so please just trust me here with this request." I believe we have enough of a relationship to get through this. Sure, we've had our ups and downs, but still—we can do this. I want her to let me move through my past stuff. I wasn't given that space.

ME: When you weren't given space, what was your response?

HIM: I pulled back.

ME: What happened when you pulled back?

HIM: It didn't work, or rather it didn't work for both of us. I only took care of myself. Ironically, I pulled back in order not to make a bigger mess.

ME: Thank you. I see your intention about it. Then what happened?

HIM: I told her, "I'm in the middle of something here. I need time to dive into it." For me, that was a clear request. I can't attend to out there when I need to be in here.

ME: You asked for space and time. And when it didn't happen, what did you do?

HIM: I became more insistent.

ME: Let's **observe** together. What do we see and hear?

HIM: He says to her, "You're not giving me what I want."

ME: And therefore…

HIM: You're wrong. Fix it. Get over it. Leave me alone.

ME: Could your message be summarized as "I'm not getting what I want and you're the cause of my difficulties"?

HIM: Yes. That was my mindset.

ME: Then she must leave you alone like you asked, right? But what if she doesn't?

HIM: I get loud. And, in a way, it works.

ME: Yes, it works in the sense she's more likely to leave you alone if you threaten her. But for it to continue to work, you must stay angry and control the situation through force and dominance.

HIM: That's what I do now. And I don't like that. It's not good for me. It's not good for us. I grew up in a loud, angry household. I want something different than that.

ME: To address your request to find "what else you've got," I'll pretend to be her now, and represent her as accurately as I can in the role she played with you recently. Okay?

HIM: Sure.

Are You Leaving Me?

ME: Here I am, your beautiful woman, and I'm happy 'cause we're spending this special week together before you leave for a month. Then surprise, surprise—you come home with an announcement that you need space and time. You don't say much, so I prod a little because, after all, you've awakened my inner CaveWoman out of a dead sleep. I'm suddenly scared. Have I lost you? Was it something I said? Why don't you talk to me? Or touch me? Have you tossed me to the tigers? Am I on my own now?

HIM: Where did you come up with the idea that I might leave you?

ME: Because you aren't as friendly. You don't smile. You're buttoned up. More solitary. You walk differently. You don't talk to me as much as before, and when you do speak, your speech patterns are different. They are more calculated, not intimate. You avoid me. You aren't as confident or funny or carefree. You're not lighthearted like you were yesterday. You don't include me. You don't look into my eyes. Where'd you go? When will you come back? You haven't told me anything that would calm me down. I'm terrified. [There's a long pause.] Shall I go on? You've given me a load of signals that you might leave. In a way, you've already left.

HIM: Oh. Okay. That's impressive. That's an amazing list. And it's probably all true. I had no idea I communicated all that.

ME [gesturing to his girlfriend]: She reads your face. Your body. Your sound. Your movements. She's concluded that things are alarmingly different. She feels unsafe.

HIM: Okay. I'm astonished.

ME: Normally, you'd look over at me in a way that would make me feel seen. Included. Cared about. If you were "normal you," you'd recognize my fear. You'd take me into your arms. Something must be wrong if you're not doing that. I want to support your inner exploration, but to succeed, I've got to rein in my fear. I'm sending distress signals. Can you please give me reasons to calm down? We could trade. You give me information, and in return I'll give you space to reflect. This could work for both of us.

HIM: But there was so much turmoil going on with me. How am I supposed to see over there to her?

ME: You had already gone into "inner mode." Nothing is wrong with what you did. This is about seeing what might work better in the future.

HIM: Okay, I can do that.

ME: To find what might work better next time, we step back to **observe**. How did it go? What were your actions? What were hers? And so on. We'll **reflect** on your **observations,** and we'll find benefit. All of this will fortify your relationship.

HIM: Okay, I'm good with that. Keep going.

ME: What may have terrified her is that you indicated she was not included in your process.

HIM: How would I include her? I can't imagine how to do that.

ME: How about something like "I can see that my request has caused stress in you. Let's talk about this over dinner tonight. I love you, and this will be fine." By offering this, you own your reaction and recognize hers as well. At dinner, you may be able to say to her, "My request is that you give me time to think things through about my past so I can be a better partner to you."

HIM: Sounds good.

When Your CavePerson Takes Over

ME: Let's clarify your trigger reactions to each other.

> *During Mouse-in-the-Corner, I take a visual and emotional check on the silent partner. I do that now. She's comfortable and alert. She's doing fine. She also knows that I know, which is important.*

ME [to him]: With the request for time to ponder, you activated her CaveWoman. I'm about to exaggerate in order to make a point. Bottom line is that you said to her, "You don't matter to me right now. My plan is to save myself. Off I go to hibernate, and after that, I won't see you for a month. You're on your own for a while. Wild tigers may get you, but oh well. That's the way it goes."

To logical, reasonable you, this is an overstatement, but not to CaveFolks. Survival Selves are pretty drastic. If you throw me out of the cave—or I *think* you have—I'm left to fend for myself. I'm not a nice girl when I'm upset about my survival. I'll fight for my place in the cave—in your life. I don't care what I have to do or for how long I have to do it. I'll use drama, tears, et cetera. Which is what I did, right?

HIM: Yes. Exactly. That's actually what happened.

ME: If you make my Survival Self afraid, you'll bring out the absolute worst in me. And then I'll feel terrible about myself 'cause I'm needy. I don't want to feel that way. Please help me.

> *She is now bawling without restraint. He's hyper-aware of her emotional response, that she apparently resonates with what I said about her. His lights are going on.*

ME [to her]: How am I doing on your behalf?

> *She gives a blubbery thumbs-up and cries louder. Her feelings and reactions have been described to him in a way he can*

understand. Plus, she is understood. By me. By him. By herself. What a relief. She's got two big wads of Kleenex, one in each hand, up to her face. She's letting her fear unravel.

How Can He Include Her?

ME [turning back to him]: So how might you turn things around next time?

HIM: I could be physically closer to her. Go to her, touch her.

ME: That would help. Could you hug her?

HIM: Probably not.

ME: Thank you for your honesty. I appreciate that. But, as you said, you could touch her.

HIM: I could also talk more, tell her more. I could learn to do that.

ME: Doing that would go a long way.

> *He considers this, and when he shifts, we continue. I'll ask him how he might offer her more information.*

ME: Okay. I'm still here, your beautiful woman. How can you learn to tell me more? How might you include me in your process?

HIM: I don't know. I really have no idea.

ME: What could you say so that I can give you time to work through your past?

HIM: I just don't know...

ME: Go ahead and try something. We'll make good use of whatever you propose.

HIM: Okay, how about this. Something has come up. I know you expect this week to be full of wonderful experiences, but I need to take some time right now to discover things about myself.

ME: That's a great start. I especially like the part, "I know you expect this week to be full of wonderful experiences..." To say "something has come up" tends to sound ominous, though, as in mysterious and probably bad. Does this mean you're having second thoughts about me? Us? Will you start this new job miles away and never speak to me again? Remember, you need to say something to calm my Survival Self.

ME [turning to her briefly]: Am I still doing okay on your behalf?

HER [blowing her nose]: Yes, you're saying my words! I feel you IN ME!

ME [to her]: Okay. Good. [back to him] "What else could it be" is a muscle most of us don't use often enough. To explore this is quite revealing, wouldn't you say?

HIM: Yes, I'm a little surprised I can't seem to conjure up anything else. I don't know. How about this: "I am churned up about some topics discussed in my session with Terri..."

ME: Such as...

HIM: ...about my past relationships with women. I want some time to work through that.

ME: So that...

HIM: So that I show up better here.

ME: Yes, exactly! Yes! So that you can be a better partner with me, hallelujah and OMG! What a difference that would make! I'd give you time for that! I'd leave you alone! I want you to finish that old stuff. Heck yes, do what you gotta do! This message from you would save her from anguish and worry and—big bonus—you'd get her support. That's pretty effective, don't you think? [He nods.] You've included me and relaxed me. I'm aware of your intentions. So helpful!

You may recall that earlier in this conversation, I handed him the thought that time to himself would contribute to being a better partner. But it wasn't his idea. He needed to find the answer for himself.

Calming Down Our Survival Selves

HIM: But it seems like you can't really do anything about CaveWoman.

ME: Actually, we can do a great deal about our Survival Selves. Women can console CaveWoman and evolve her. We can be aware of CaveWoman's presence, and then, bit by bit, talk her down from any cliff.

Our Survival Selves are not the best of us. Over time, you'll begin to recognize when your CavePerson takes over. You'll deal more skillfully with your angry CaveMan. If you did for your sweetheart what we're suggesting here, you'd have a different woman in the house. You'd have the one you like.

They both burst into laughter, even though she's in Mouse-in-the-Corner.

ME: Even better, you'd have the one *she likes!*

She raises both arms overhead and gives two thumbs up! I love when people break rules in key moments. Things are loosening up! From now on we'll be in a relaxed version of Mouse-in-the-Corner. You'll see how beautifully this works.

ME: If CaveWoman is reassured, then your sweetheart can give you time to deal with your past. Do you agree with that?

237

HIM: I think so.

ME: Oh, I think she wholeheartedly respects and trusts that you need time for that—and she would gladly give it to you!

HER [breaking Mouse-in-the-Corner silence]: I DO trust that!

ME [to him]: When she's afraid, she needs more words from you than you're inclined to give. There's a bit of a dance here. Each time you step toward her—give more words—you reinforce your partnership. Her part of this step-toward dance is to give you room to process your past. Do you see the dance?

They both nod.

ME: There's nothing wrong here. Your relationship is not in trouble. What happened is that your Survival Selves took the helm. The moment you recognize them and give a simple nod to say "I see you," your CavePeople will stand down. You'll get your real relationship back.

It's obvious they like this idea.

ME: Next, what does she need in order to give you what you need? Is that a question you might be able to ask her?

HIM: I'm not sure about the wording.

ME: How would you say it?

HIM: "Is there anything else you need so that I can take this time for myself?"

ME: Beautiful. That works. [At the same moment, we both look over at her, and she nods.]

ME [to him]: And what if later she pushes for information, even though you asked her not to?

HIM: I could say, "I respect that this is a problem for you, but I need this time to be a better partner with you."

ME: That might work. Can you simplify it even more?

Again, we look over to get a suggestion from her.

HER: Maybe "Please hear me," or, "Please hear my request." It would be even better if I got the word "sweetie" along with the request. You know, you could hold up your hand and say, "Sweetie, I can't go there." That would do it for me.

HIM: Okay, good.

The two of them smile at each other. Then they realize their love is all lit up, and they both laugh. And yes, we're in that relaxed version of Mouse-in-the-Corner mentioned previously.

HER: Wow, this is the first time we've looked directly at each other in days!

*He reaches for her hand. She **receives** him.*

ME: I love when humans fall in love again in this room! It's my favorite thing! All right. What now? Anything else?

~~~~~

We covered a great deal but we're not done. Next is part two of our session.

~~~~~

A happy marriage is the union of two good forgivers.
—Ruth Bell Graham

25

Conversation: Two Angry People Find Love Again, Part 2

THE CONVERSATION CONTINUES.

~~~~~

HER: It's better than it used to be, but his anger is still a problem—the sudden snap, the push against me. His pop-up wrath affects the trust in our relationship.

ME [to him]: Okay, I'm going to offer you time to integrate while I work with her.

HER: Wait! I'm not the only one involved in this.

ME: We'll approach this as if you are the only one, because you're the one asking for help. As long as you see him as the bad guy who yells at you, things won't change.

HER: Yeah…right now I kind of hate that…

ME: I know…

We pause until she signals to go on. He's given me thumbs-up about being in Mouse-in-the-Corner.

ME: Why does he get angry so often?

HER: I have no idea. It comes out of nowhere.

Interesting! She's back to how things come out of the blue. Apparently, there's more to do about it.

ME: Maybe it doesn't come out of nowhere.

Oh, mama. Her temperature is risin'.

ME: If you believe his anger comes out of nowhere, there's nothing you can do about it. You have no influence.

HER: It DOES come out of nowhere! The other night I asked him to come to the bedroom and be with me, and it was like...[I hold up my hand like a stop sign]

I don't interrupt often when a client speaks, but after we've worked on a topic for a while, I may stop the train as I do here. At this point in her work with me, her job is to catch herself. My interruption models what I'm asking her to do: just stop in the middle of a rant. Stop the presses. Call it off. She can do this. And now, even though I thought this would be integration time for him, my inclination is to ask him for information.

ME: Hold on. I must consult him.

HER: Okay.

ME [to him]: May I interrupt Mouse-in-the-Corner with a question?

HIM: Sure. I'm fine with that.

Time for Dinner

ME: How does your irritation typically start?

HIM: Here's what happened just the other day. I know she meant well, but to me it was like "What the hell…?!" I was focused on an email, and here comes a plate shoved in my face. It was dinner she prepared. She sticks the plate in my face and says, "Here." She could have put it next to me. There was room. So, I did stop working on the email, then said, "Just put it right there." I wanted to get the email done and be available.

> *With this description from him, her emotions escalate. That she is willing to be seen is a beautiful and generous gesture on her part.*

ME [back to her]: Okay, let's solve this plate-in-the-face matter.

HER: I said, "It's time for dinner." I had two plates in my hands. I didn't know about his important email. And there wasn't room to set down a plate next to him.

> *It's official. We're out of Mouse-in-the-Corner now. It's okay. We're flexible.*

HIM: She could have set it on top of her closed laptop.

ME: Most likely she didn't consider that space for a plate.

HER: No, I wouldn't put it there. It's not space.

ME [to him]: So, did you take the plate and put it on her computer?

HIM: No, I took it and put it over on the table.

ME: And you were angry?

HIM: Yes, my temper was short because I was in the midst of typing. I was focused, trying to wrap up. I thought, "What!?! Just let me finish, and then I'll sit with you."

I need to know more about his fury. I don't really know how he reacts to her in his coldest CaveMan ways. He's never shown me in a session. My intention now is to engage his CaveMan in order to witness what she's confronted with at home. I'm aware it won't be pretty.

ME: Okay, she didn't realize that you were writing an email, right?

HIM [turning critical and cold]: It was obvious she hadn't bothered to notice.

ME: Is there any way you could have given her the benefit of the doubt at that moment?

HIM: As in what?

ME: She loves you. She's got food in her hands. She's made dinner for you. This is an act of generosity, don't you think? Knowing her as I do, it was probably food she made herself.

HIM: Right, actually, it was.

ME: Okay, so one might possibly look at your reaction and say, "What an asshole!"

That pushed his anger button. He will show us what she experiences when he gets angry. The priority, though, is that I want him to give us the part of him he doesn't like and doesn't respect. If he can give it to us, it will no longer be a secret, awful thing that happens in private. When a man's most crass CaveMan is seen and understood and still he is loved and respected, he experiences unconditional love. Then there's no going back. To reveal his undeveloped aspect and be loved

243

anyway will change him. She'll watch me, and it will help her, too. Layers of learning will occur in the next few minutes. (Note: Don't try this at home. It takes experience and practice.) He is instantly angered by my comment that he could be seen as an asshole and turns scary-cold-as-ice.

HIM: And I could respond by saying equally, "You're a f★★★-ing b★★★★! Be aware of someone else!!!!"

All right then! Mission accomplished! His anger is nasty. No surprise there. But now it's out in the open. He gave it to us. What we witnessed was possibly a more polite, controlled version of what she suffers at home. He swears, calls her names, and acts like an asshole. His CaveMan is pretty swift with his stick, undoubtedly similar to how his father's Survival Self was expressed in the presence of family.

I pushed my client into CaveMan. I'm responsible. I'll invite him back out. To get him back to center requires being genuine. I'm not pretending here or going through the motions. This is real. He let me see the part of him he's not proud of. My heart goes out to him, and because he knows me well, he probably notices. I'll do three things to pull him out of his Neanderthal reflexes fast:

- *One, I'll speak in facts and logic, which will calm him.*
- *Two, I'll validate him, which will usher him back to center.*
- *And three, I'll put him in control. I'll make a request and give him a clear option to refuse.*

ME [step one, use fact and logic]: So it's a fact that you were focused on the email and had no thought about dinner. Is that correct?

HIM [sternly]: Yes. I was busy.

ME [step two, validate him]: You were concentrating on the task. Being focused is a good thing. It's one of your strong suits. You do it well.

He relaxes more, and I can feel his inner CaveMan (thankfully) lowering the giant hunting stick.

ME [step three, put him in control]: Would it be all right to talk about CaveMan and CaveWoman in conversation with each other and learn more about how they relate? Does that work for you?

HIM [calm now]: Okay. That's fine with me.

> *My question ("does that work for you?") gives him options. He can refuse. He can talk about something else. He can bow out for a while and take a break, or leave the session, even. He's back in control.*

> *To walk any man out of CaveMan is a kindness. My client doesn't realize how quickly he becomes CaveMan, and neither does he know how to recover or do better next time. (In the future, I'll go over details with both of them about what happened. We'll **breathe, receive, observe,** and **reflect** about CaveMan's ways when he's not in the middle of it.) The other clear advantage here is that with some assistance, he can realize "what else he has besides anger." Alternatives to anger are a clear priority for him, and I'm committed to delivering on his request.*

CaveMan's Reaction to Interruptions

ME: Let's tell this "dinner plate in my face" story in CaveMan, CaveWoman terms. You're a hunter, and you've got your bow and arrow aimed at that last email. You're focused and within range, poised for a perfect shot. Then, lo and behold, there's a ruckus, a distraction coming from the bushes. It's your girlfriend holding baskets of food she collected. She's offering a meal. She's unaware that she's about to mess up your chances of nailing the target—killing your last email. She's taking you off your game, yes?

HIM: For sure! Heck yes! Exactly!

ME: Which is not your favorite thing at all, Mr. CaveMan! So, what do you do? What are your options? Turn your bow and arrow and slay the distraction—your girlfriend—so you can hit the target, finish the email?

> *He mulls this over. If Caveman can't accomplish his goal, he'll eliminate the distraction that prevents the completion of his objective. My client does this by aiming angry words at his girlfriend. He gets cold as ice, swears, and calls her names. He silences her through fear. He now sees this (and so does she).*

HIM: I want to do this differently, but I have no idea how.

ME: When a hunter is focused, one of his least favorite things is to be interrupted. Why?

HIM: 'Cause he can't get his job done.

ME: What will you do?

HIM: That's the piece...I don't really know what to do about that.

ME: Do you recognize when you're about to say harsh words? Do you sense when you're about to snap into "angry and cold"?

HIM: In some cases I do.

> *He starts to smile, then laughs outright. He's about to go on a valuable tangent rather than answer my question.*

HIM: She has the uncanny ability to know when I'm in the bathroom. She'll just have to talk to me right then! She's gotta ask me a question!

ME: Ha! She has a radar! She knows when you're sitting still.

HIM [still laughing]: Is there a way to turn that radar off?

ME: No, not in our home.

HIM: It's comic in a way.

ME: Yes, but our radar is what gives us the ability to take care of the people we love. If you're in the house, our radar is on. If you're upset, our radar picks up on it.

HIM: That's true. I grew up in a household with an asshole and a bitch and never knew when I was about to be smacked in the back of the head or beaten or whatever. I know what it's like to keep the radar up so you can get the hell out of the way.

ME: Yes. That's a survival radar alert to potential threats. That's one important type. There is a feminine version. If things are safe, our radar scans the environment to see what or who needs to be nurtured. Who is hungry? Who is thirsty? Are the plants watered? Dog fed? Do the children need a nap? [We chat about this.]

A Key to Evolving Our Survival Selves

ME: Let's head back to the plate-in-the-face incident. What are your options when she interrupts you?

HIM: One option is to stop what I was doing.

ME: Yes. And you did that, actually. But what about your reaction to stopping?

HIM: I could say, "Would you please set that plate over there?"

ME: But here's the thing. And this, I believe, is often the missing piece between two people who love each other. What could you say as she stands with two plates of fresh food that will move you toward her, and her toward you?

HIM: I could say, "I'll be done in just a moment, and then I can join you."

ME: Yes, great. Can you evolve your CaveMan even further?

He looks quizzical. She sits on the edge of her seat, speculating about possible answers.

HIM: No clue. Hints, please.

ME: What if you were able to say to her, "Thank you, that looks delicious" as your opening remark?

HIM: I'm not sure how I would manage to say that. Sorry, but that's honest.

ME: Do you see the power in those words, though? To first see the good in her actions and say thank you is a gesture that walks toward her. It builds a bridge.

HIM: I do see that. But that will take some practice.

ME: I'm sure that's true. In your childhood home, was there expression of gratitude?

HIM: That was rare or nonexistent.

ME: So you didn't learn how to speak gratitude there. Can you learn it now? [He nods.] By the way, the part where you reach out to her—"Thank you, that looks delicious"—is in the category of bonus points.

His face lights up with a broad smile. He says he loves bonus points!

ME: I thought you might! Being kind brings out the best in both of you. Plus it gets bonus points! Expressing authentic appreciation is really efficient.

Get ready for what he says next. He's about to share with you the power of CaveMan.

HIM: And you know what? The really silly thing is that I had three words left to type on the email. Not much left to do. I just wanted to finish.

ME: Amazing! Three words left to type! That's the power of our Survival Selves! [We sit a few moments in silence to **receive** the wonder of his confession.] You can teach your CaveMan: "Hey, I've got three words left to type. Sit tight while I turn to this beautiful woman and thank her for the food she's prepared." That is, if you want to forge a new path for yourself, one that's different from how your father and mother treated each other.

There is a collective sigh as this piece settles in. We get up and take a break. This has grown into quite a session.

~~~~~

The conversation resumes and completes in the next chapter.

~~~~~

Appreciation is a wonderful thing.
It makes what is excellent in others belong to us as well.
—Voltaire

26

Conversation: Two Angry People
Find Love Again, Part 3

THE CONVERSATION CONTINUES.

~~~~~

ME: Is there anything else on your mind before we wrap up?

> *She dives in without hesitation. This is a safe space, and she intends to use it to her advantage. I check whether he's okay to continue, and he nods.*

HER: He tells me, "Stop making a story." He says I talk too much. When I share what goes on in my life, sometimes he shuts me up by saying, "I'm sorry you're choosing to feel this way."

ME: Good. Since you're both on board, we'll address the new question on the table.

> *Note to reader: Specific suggestions around listening and venting are sourced from the work of Alison Armstrong.*

ME [to him]: I'll represent your point of view as best I can, though my style is to use more words than you would. Please stop me if I'm not accurate. [He nods.] Here we go.

ME [to her, speaking as him]: Sometimes I have no idea how to listen to you. When you tell a long story about what happened at work, it overwhelms me. You dive into the conversation and give me nonstop information, full of emotion, too, with no instructions for how to listen to you. What's the purpose of this conversation? What kind of assistance do you need?

HER: I'm not asking for help. I just want to talk.

ME: Well, I want to know your problem. Then I can help you fix it. But when you pile on more details, I get angry, because I don't want these words from you unless I know how I can be of assistance. Otherwise, what's the point of having a conversation?

HER: Seriously...? Are you kidding me...? Can't you just listen?

ME [shaking my head slowly]: No point, no goal—that's lame.

HER: What...???

ME: I love you. I want to support you by making your life better— make your trouble disappear—so why would I listen and do nothing? My brain is a lean, mean, problem-solving machine. Let's put it to work.

> *She sits in silence with her mouth partway open. She begins to speak but considers again what was said. Finally, she looks over at him and cocks her head as if to say, "Is what Terri says true???" He smiles but remains silent. He wants to see what happens next. He's enjoying this. She is intrigued by his playful "let's see where this goes" attitude.*

ME [to her]: Shall I say more?

HER: Yes. I don't understand this. At all.

ME: Ask me a question so I know how to help you.

HER: I don't get the part about how he can't just listen to me.

ME: He listens to you differently than you listen to him.

HER: Okay, like what? Please go over that again.

ME: The masculine listens with purpose—to find the point or the problem.

> *Remember the previous discussion where we can access our "other side"? Women can access their masculine side and listen to find the point or the problem, and certain men vent. The key is to be aware of what we do now and then expand our skill set. I'm asking her to do this.*

ME: It's kind to tell him how he could be useful to you in the conversation. How do you want him to listen? Are you looking for solutions, for instance? Will you want his input at the end of your story? If so, what kind of input? Or, do you want him in listen-only mode? Ask for it.

ME [to him]: How am I doing? Does this represent you?

HIM: It's good. The main reason I want to help her fix things is that she's clearly suffering, and I want her to stop suffering.

ME: Ah! Exactly! Thank you.

HIM: She's in a negative swirl, so let's get her out of there. I personally couldn't stay there. I'd fight to get out of that hole.

ME: Well, just so you know, venting her feelings helps get her out of the hole.

HIM: [smiling] Okay. But...how much venting does one need?

ME: Well, most likely she needs way too much for your tastes! You might need to hold up your hand and tell her when you've had enough.

HIM [laughing heartily]: Oh, you don't want me to say, "STOP! I can't take it anymore!"

> *I love that he's back to playful. And I play back. But I want to drive home a couple of important ideas, so I thank him for his lightheartedness here and then lock eyes with him.*

ME: Two important points, okay?

HIM [still laughing]: Okay. I'm all ears. I promise.

ME [looking at him and pointing to her]: She might not know when you can't take it anymore. Let her know.

ME [looking at her and pointing to him]: He doesn't listen to you like another woman would. Vent less to him. And when you do vent, give instructions. Do you want his help with a problem? If so, what kind? Whatever you need, tell him why that would be valuable. Watch for signs he's had enough: his eyes will glaze over, his interest will fade, or he'll look for an "out." His actions will say, "Babe, I gotta go."

ME [looking at him and pointing to her]: If she could snap her fingers and feel better fast, she would. She's smart that way. You listen with purpose, and she vents with purpose. She vents to clear her emotions and get to empty. When she's empty—open, available, present—she's at her best. And because you don't experience the value of venting, you want her to stop. Please know that if she's venting, she's already off-center, and if you add criticism on top of it, that's really hard.

HIM: I see it now. [He turns to her.] I'm sorry.

HER: It's okay. I'm new at this, too.

This mutual apology is a tender moment between them. We savor it, then move to her final question.

HER: I want to talk about one last thing. He's about to move to another state, and he plans to buy a house where we could live together. He has actually told me that going down there is not about disconnection, but after he disappeared into his private process and wouldn't talk to me, I just didn't believe him anymore!

ME: Would you like to live where he is going?

HER: No. And not just no. Hell no!

Uproarious laughter ensues.

ME: Maybe you have two homes?

HER: Hmm. That could work. I would consider my home to be here and my vacation to be there. I could do that. As a matter of fact, I even like that idea!

ME: Can you say more about why you like it?

HER: The fuddy-duddy-homebody part of me is a real troublemaker, but once I change things up, I love it. It can require an act of Congress to get me out of town or out to dinner or whatever. But this idea of having two homes and a change of scene is a really good way to deal with my fuddy-duddy. I like the anticipation of being with him, what I'll take with me, what I'll wear. I love when he makes the hotel and dinner reservations. It's quality time together with no distractions.

ME: Great! Is there anything else before we wrap this up?

HER [turning to him with a soft smile]: So you're not breaking up with me?

HIM: No, sweetheart. I'm all in.

Their fondness for one another overflows as his hand slides over to hers.

ME: Thank you both. What a good session. Are we complete?

They nod.

~~~~~

In this session, we used core skills at every turn. This couple breathed through anger and were able to activate the combined wisdom of their brain and heart. They also received. They took in, listened, and relaxed enough to become curious. They both stepped back to observe facts. How did their reaction start, what was it made of, and what did they learn from it? And they reflected. They found benefit in what had been a stressful situation. They have plenty of new actions and understandings to rehearse.

This was also a profound lesson in the power of our Survival Selves. When our Survival Selves take the reins, we lose the best of our relationship to fear, worry, and scarcity. We get back the good when breathe, receive, observe, reflect and rehearse.

When I vented to Eric, sometimes I suggested in advance that it would likely be a thought-blurt—no need to listen, but if I heard something golden coming out of my mouth, I'd remember it, and we could talk about it later. That worked for us. But at some point I stopped venting to him. It was unnecessary. Alternately, I chose a female friend, or I worked it out internally. Sometimes I wrote in on paper. All of this suited me, but I've had a great deal of practice. Whether you vent to an empty room or to a trusted person, listen for what's essential for you.

Getting to know our ancient selves helps a relationship work more smoothly. Our CaveFolks usually scrap with one another from a place of scarcity or fear. One antidote to Cave-related issues is generosity. To offer a thank-you or to hold space for another's point of view—these are powerful forms.

One simple, generous act that Eric practiced regularly involved football games on TV. When I walked into the room, he paused the TV instantly and looked up to see whether there was a question or a need. I never asked him to do this, but it touched me each time he did it. It was a direct message from him that said "You matter to me." When he broke his focus and included me, I felt him walk toward me, which was not only kind, but his gesture invited me to walk toward him. How smart. How sexy. How loving.

Reaching toward your partner with generosity because it's your desire, and because you know how, matters. Harmony and respect keep the embers of your relationship lit and burning bright.

~~~~~

> This is the time to fly, to create, to investigate,
> to listen, to invent together.
> —Bayo Akomolafe

Along comes a second chance.
What will you do with it?

27

Conversation: Second Chances

THIS IS ANOTHER conversation where the rubber meets the road, where core skills are put to use in practical ways. Prior to sessions with me, this couple separated for a year, and then got back together. The part of the conversation shared here is with the woman, because she highlights issues common to relationships undergoing renovation. I'll emphasize these in the narration. In addition, there is the overarching question of how she'll take advantage of this second chance for a better marriage. Again, references to the five core skills are in bold font.

~~~~

HER: Things are out of whack. And I'm exhausted spiritually, emotionally, physically. I'm beyond tired. I've given up.

ME: Thank you. And how are the two of you?

HER: We're five steps back. He doesn't communicate with me. There are things I want to discuss, and maybe we speak for half a second, but nothing comes of it. Things stay the same. It doesn't matter what I try. I can hint about the need for sincere communication, insist on it, or hand him a long letter full of why. Nothing works. I did actually hand him a long letter when other attempts to connect failed. He didn't respond to it until I finally said, "So, did you read the letter?" He acknowledged it, but we didn't address what I said in the note. We lie in bed together, but we're separate. I don't feel loved. I don't feel important.

ME: This is your button, right? Not feeling important?

HER: So it hurts. When he makes a joke out of what's important to me, that doesn't work! We're in a relationship. We have to communicate. I'm not complaining, but not being able to talk doesn't work.

> *She speaks in earnest now, and her voice has shifted to a forceful tone.*

ME: Actually, maybe you are complaining right now?

HER: Well, maybe I *sound* like I'm complaining...

> *Before things get rolling, let's press pause for a note about sound and voice. Even when a female's voice doesn't sound like music to a male's ears, his brain thinks it is. The part of the male brain that processes a female's voice is the same part that processes music. This could explain a few things!*

> *The study: "Psychiatrist Michael Hunter and fellow researchers at the University of Sheffield in England monitored the brain activity of 12 men as they listened to voice recordings and found they process male voices differently from those of females. Women's voices stimulate an area of the brain used for processing complex sounds, like music. Male voices activate the 'mind's eye,' a region of the brain used for conjuring imagery."[32] The study went on to say that a woman's speaking voice generally has more variation in melody than a man's speaking voice.*

> *If a female voice sounds like good music, a male brain pays attention and decodes the message. But if a female voice sounds like bad music, he turns it off (tunes her out). How we sound matters!*

The woman in session with me does what many of us do. When frustrated, we put dissatisfaction into our voice for extra punch. This, however, makes us harder to hear. We sound like bad music, and our message gets tuned out.

After a review of this idea, I asked my client to restate her request from a more centered place. She did so, which naturally changed her vocal tone. This made all the difference for her and for him as well. She felt better about her clean request. He also heard her.

Women, in the interest of efficiency, self-esteem, and most of all, love, remember your sound is not speech; it's music! Now, back to the conversation.

ME: Your voice has an edge to it. Can you hear it?

HER: Yes.

*I am asking her to **observe**.*

ME: We hear your words, but what does your tone communicate?

HER: That I'm upset. There are some things bothering me. I'm asking him to talk to me.

ME: What are you saying with your energy as you speak?

HER: That he should do what I've asked him to do.

ME: Would you say there's urgency from you? Pressure? [She nods.] Why?

HER: Because I need what I'm asking for.

ME: Yes, and why do you need it?

HER: I don't know. I just need it.

ME: If you got your wish, what would that do for you?

HER: I'd feel better.

ME: Then are you saying to him, "Please change for me so I can feel better"?

HER: I am.

ME: What if you first did the work of feeling better and then asked him to talk with you?

HER: But I don't feel better until I get what I want.

ME: So does that mean how you feel is his responsibility?

HER: Obviously, I can't control him.

ME: If he doesn't do what you ask, then what?

HER: I'm stuck. Therefore, he should fix it.

ME: Just wondering here…What if fixing how you feel is not his job?

HER [spitting her words]: So when I have a conversation with my husband about an issue, he shouldn't respond to me? He should ignore me?

ME [with compassion]: No. That's not my message here. You've told me you want satisfying conversations with your husband, but you're not getting them. How about taking a new road?

> *How do I know her methods don't fly? Because she has told me. She described how they are "five steps back" and that she's*

261

exhausted. Even with her increased vocal volume and emotional pressure, nothing changes.

He would prefer to be able to talk with her. He has expressed it many times. They have a strong connection, and they enjoy so many things about each other. But she's angry and hurt. This will take some time. We continue.

HER: I'm about to explode about this. I'm tired of it all. I have so many things going for me, but my partner wants no part of me. When he moved back home after we separated, my palms started to sweat because I was excited about being with him again. But then the excitement went away. I'm really tired. [She bursts into tears.]

ME: I see that.

*I hold her hand as she releases emotion (**receive** her), and we talk a bit. I'm about to ask her for facts about her situation. This will help her get to acceptance.*

ME: Are you ready to explore? [She nods.] What was it like when he came back home?

HER: There was a nice energy from him. He was open. He quit playing moody music and stopped hiding from me.

ME: Thank you. What happened with you? How were you different?

HER: I was more open, freer, softer.

ME: How did you get that way?

HER: I don't know. I just did it. It was comfortable and natural, and it felt good. I don't think I did anything unusual.

She has highlighted a vital point here: it's easier to feel loving and loved in an environment that is supportive, rather than in one that challenges. It's a breeze to express ourselves or get what we need when interactions are packed with positivity. When a partner is open and attentive, we bathe in the affection, and it brings out the best of us.

But what happens when our partnership environment isn't sweet and easy? When things are less favorable, we're challenged to provide what's missing, what's needed. For instance, without approval from our mate, we can supply self-approval. If compassion seems absent, we can furnish that. The great irony is that difficult people press us to grow. They push us—even force us—to expand our skill sets.

The woman in this conversation doesn't yet know how to summon resourcefulness when her circumstances are problematic. When she doesn't get positive attention, cooperation, or loving words from her husband, she blames him for the lack and for her unhappiness.

She doesn't create a consistently positive flow between the two of them, because she doesn't create this positive flow for herself. And no, neither does her husband. They are a match. It takes only one person to turn it around, and she's the one asking for assistance.

Observe *her with me for a moment. When things don't go her way, what does she do? What is her habit?*

She hopes that telling him what she wants or telling him more often or louder will summon a solution. She complains, hoping he'll change. But he doesn't. He turns off the bad music and vanishes, leaving her frustrated, exhausted, and alone.

*What can shift, if she's willing? When she gets frustrated about not getting what she wants from her husband, she can take a moment to **breathe** and get to a place of acceptance (**receive**). From a calm place, she can make a clear request and be heard. She is also more likely to remember to approve of herself even if he doesn't. She will be able to speak from her center even if her husband loses his.*

She can do her best to come into her day from unwavering love and appreciation. She can stand in love, come from love, be love. By doing this, she becomes what she is looking for from her mate. The love she seeks is within her. It's what she's made of. There's no need to blame her husband for a lack of something she possesses in abundance. This love of hers (for her) will also change him. He will feel more free to be the love he's made of.

Now back to the conversation, and to the question at hand: how did she improve things when her husband moved back home after their separation?

How Does Your Story Go?

ME: But here's the thing. You behaved differently, saw him in a new way—something! How did you influence the situation in a positive way?

HER: I have no idea what I did. I mean, I listened. I was involved.

ME: What about your frame of mind?

HER: Well, I was excited. I was open to the good possibilities our second chance might bring.

ME: You were open, fresh, and new. How brilliant! That's a powerful step. What else did you do that was favorable?

HER: When he came back home, that made me feel important.

ME: Your problem of not feeling important was taken care of. Your husband provided a loving environment where your problem didn't show up. This doesn't mean you took care of your issue. It was left sitting right where you left it. Do you see that?

HER: Yes.

ME: And then gradually what happened?

HER: Things went back to the way they were before we separated. I wanted to talk and relate, and he made jokes about it... [She trails off.]

ME: What if you would begin to take care of feeling important?

I pause to observe how the question I asked earlier sits with her in this new moment. Something has shifted, but I can't quite tell what it is.

ME: What if you faced your issue and did your work? What if you addressed the idea that feeling important is yours to do?

HER [suddenly laughing]: That...sounds...terrible...!

ME: I know, right?!?!? Heaven forbid we should take responsibility for ourselves! Do you know what I love the most about your style?

I smile as she waits in anticipation for the answer. After a few moments she signals that I should disclose it.

ME: I love that you're thorough.

She groans and laughs at the same time, and shakes her head.

HER: Well, I think I'm thoroughly good at producing bad results. It's my specialty.

ME: Do you wish to develop a new specialty?

HER [flippantly]: Oh sure, why not? [Then she relaxes a bit.] But in all sincerity, yes, I'd like to find a new specialty.

ME: How might you do that?

HER: Please help me get started.

ME: Here's a fundamental idea. You decide that the quality of your relationship with your husband is up to you. You're the CEO of Your Relationship. Your husband may shift right away, or never. You're working with yourself, because you're the source of your happiness and satisfaction. When your experience of yourself changes, that changes everything.

There was the happy part where things between the two of you began to go well, and you left the past in the past. You were excited that he came back home, and you expected positive things. You felt free and open. Dinners together were fun, and you talked to each other. Then what? Tell me how things changed.

> *I've simplified her answers in this next section as if she named them one by one. It actually required some discussion to get to each one.*

HER: I judged his words and actions. I became cold. I didn't get many hugs, but when they did come, I didn't hug back. Not really.

ME: Thank you. What else?

HER: Oh, probably a lot of things. I stopped giving him the time of day. I kept my love for him in check. I expressed disdain, let him know when I wasn't pleased. I acted out my negative emotions. Made him pay. Punished him.

ME: How does your story go? Share with me the pattern you **rehearse**.

HER: Well, I start out happy, and things are great. I'm mellow, I smile a lot, and I'm eager. I believe good things will happen. And good things do happen. My husband and I talk. We hold hands. We go out to dinner, enjoy each other's company. We plan for the future. We laugh, have great vacations. We find great delight in watching our children find their way in the world.

ME: And then?

266

HER: And then I guess I get sloppy. It's like when someone loses weight. Once they reach their goal, they can easily go back to eating too much. It just doesn't work to go back to old ways and believe things will stay rosy. But I do.

ME: Like what? Can you be more specific about your old ways?

It is a challenge to be asked this sort of question. But as you'll see, she does well. Again, I've turned her gradual exploration into a list.

HER: My old ways. Let's see... What do I **rehearse**? I don't listen. I ignore him. I don't give my full attention. When he speaks to me, I'm busy with other things. Paperwork piles up, and I resent him for not doing it even though he's not good at paperwork. I get upset. I complain. If he doesn't help me with tasks, I make him feel bad. I expect him to know what I want with no explanation from me. I nag him regarding undone projects. I pontificate about the glass half-empty. When I don't like my life, I emphasize my dissatisfaction and insinuate that he's the cause.

What's Your Challenge?

ME: Thank you for all those ways. It's so ironic, isn't it, that you have a long-term marriage and a second chance to make it better? You have several thriving businesses, a beautiful home, great children, a long list of friends, and happy pets. You have the resources to travel and enjoy life. You are taken care of in all the basic ways people say they want to feel taken care of. What is your challenge?

HER: To realize what I have. To appreciate what I have.

ME: Yes, it's the challenge of being happy in paradise. To be joyful in a privileged life. To recognize good, celebrate it, and create more good. To amplify what's working. What are some steps you can take toward accentuating the positive?

We converse again, and here's a summary of the steps she came up with.

- Give my valuable attention to what's working, to my successes.
- Say thank you aloud more often.
- Savor my accomplishments. Talk about them. Share them.
- Use my connections and resources to finish home projects, rather than demand that either of us finish them. Hire help.
- Learn to love me so I can love him.
- Ask "is my focus on appreciation?" Appreciate first and remedy second.
- Catch and release my tendency to obsess about fault, imperfection, or incompletion.
- Ask "how can this be easy?"
- Interrupt a negative habit. Call it off. If I'm complaining, acknowledge it, and then ask myself what else I could do.

We speak about specific ways she learned to make things difficult and then practiced it for years. We explore the idea of inner housecleaning. We converse, too, about how to boost our ability to sustain joy. We speak of Dr. Rick Hanson's advice to linger in feelings of appreciation.

We recount how she was excited when her husband came home and how she nurtured the joy of that reunion. And look how things turned around! She has clear and unmistakable evidence that when she pays attention to what works, she creates ease, delight, and intimacy.

~~~~~

This couple had a fresh chance to rekindle their connection, but they soon realized that a new start does not guarantee a positive outcome. This can be confusing. She felt disappointed and disheartened, even a little betrayed, that things "got good" but didn't "stay good." It's not uncommon to think we can wrap an old package with new paper and a fresh bow and assume the contents are transformed. Lottery winners, for instance, get rich but don't often stay rich. There's the old package (themselves, their habits and beliefs) wrapped in new paper (the money). Without changes to how they relate to wealth, they go broke again. Money doesn't solve problems; it unveils them. A whopping 70 percent of lottery winners go bankrupt within a few years.[33] When this couple got back together, their second chance was similar to the lottery tale. Their joy and hope created a powerful, positive stream of activity. But eventually they invoked familiar habits and pulled their old trouble right back to them.

On the plus side, in our work together they discovered that past patterns needn't dictate future ones. Patterns can just as easily signal a choice point. A second chance beseeches us to track down old ways and unlearn them. Lucky for us, our brains are perfectly suited for overhauls. The five core skills—breathe, receive, observe, reflect, and rehearse— will continue to support her progress.

Sustained joy will feel odd to her at first, given her lifelong habit of awarding attention to what's wrong. But she's now aware of and interested in the impact of relishing successes. Her splendid circumstances will serve as great support for her!

~~~~~

Opportunities multiply as they are seized.
—Sun Tzu

28

Final Thoughts

IT IS MY deepest desire that our time together has turned you wholly toward love. As we walked and talked on these pages, I hope you grew new eyes for love, and that you see more love around you. You grew a new capacity, too, to breathe love in, and breathe it out to others. You know without a doubt that coming from love is a gift to you and to all living beings. You know love and feel the depth of it as you move through each hour, day, and year.

Only in retrospect is it possible to fathom how time with a partner molds us, how it encourages us to reimagine. Becoming aware of how we relate to others steers us toward who we truly are. Because of friendships and intimate relationships, it is possible to be forever transformed by the hand and heart of love.

My wish for you is that you continue to carry out the shifts you favor. The sign in the lobby entrance to Stanford Design School says NOTHING IS A MISTAKE. THERE IS NO WIN AND NO FAIL. THERE IS ONLY MAKE.[34] So go out there and make! Ride bareback, hair flying, arms outstretched, and call to the wind. Be the person you came here to be. Create a life you love. Let your spirit fly!

Thank you for your devotion to true-you. It makes a difference in the world to *find you, be you*. Go, darlin', go.

~~~~

Courage, dear heart.
—C.S. Lewis

ABOUT THE AUTHOR

Terri Crosby is a writer, relationship consultant, and speaker. She graduated from Iowa State University in Child Development.

For more information about available programs, study groups, classes, or private sessions for individuals and couples, visit In Care of Relationships at https://www.incareofrelationships.com/. You can contact Terri at InCareOfRelationships@gmail.com.

Terri is also the author of a book of poetry and photography called *100 Words: Small Servings of Whimsy and Wisdom to Calm the Mind and Nourish the Heart.* Each poem is 100 words long on subjects such as relationships, change, creativity, grief, and nature.

Terri lives in the breathtaking Blue Ridge Mountains of Western North Carolina and enjoys the company of nature.

ACKNOWLEDGMENTS

Thank you, Gangaji, for the many gentle and inspiring hours I've spent with you. It has made all the difference.

Thank you, William Hanrahan and Paul Baker, for voice lessons long ago, which, as it turns out, helped me in surprising and unmusical ways in the years since. William, your lessons went far beyond song. Paul, you are as magical as E. E. Cummings's bespangled clown. You are surely the reason angels play with us. My love to both of you!

Jim and Phoebe Reed, bless you for our closeness over the years and for your assistance before, during, and after Eric's passing. Giuseppe Piazza, thank you for your transformational bodywork and all the ways it supports me. Jim Weikart, my deep appreciation goes to you for lending a hand with a certain anonymous project, which freed me to pay attention to the writing of this book. You are kind and generous. To Lexi Hartman, friend and all-around brilliant person, thank you for your assistance and encouragement in the early stages of my business. To Lyte Henrickson, thank you for our time as voice class teaching partners and for our friendship. We've grown by knowing one another. Shiner Antiorio, you are an elf of the highest order, and the lilt in your laugh is uplifting at any hour. Thank you for your support of this book. Scott Tower, thank you for your friendship, kindness, and sense of humor.

Thank you, Alison Armstrong, for being a relationship mentor and beacon of hope for me and countless others. Your work was a refuge when my walls came tumbling down. You taught me new ideas, but also reminded me of what I know and what's important to me. Thank you for the afternoon in your home when you said to me, "Go out and teach your way." Your work infused me, informed me, and inspired me.

Jeff Godfrey, thank you for being you—for your clarity and integrity, for your friendship, and for your generosity in sharing who you are. Knowing you and spending time with you makes a difference to me. I'm so glad you've become a father!

Thank you, Darlene Strickland, for your inspiration, trust, and your guidance through example. You walk your talk. Tia Holmes, I love that you are the reason Eric said to me, "No, sweetheart, don't stay home. I'll be fine. Go make some trouble with Tia."

Love and appreciation to my longtime friends: Devaya Smith, Susan Gamage, Aline Autenrieth, Gary Smith, Toni Galardi, Cecile Beecroft, and Chris Hartmann. My friendship with each of you spans the years. We've seen many versions of one another. I love that you know all my versions, and hey, I know yours, too. My love for each of you spills over like a happy fountain!

To my editors. Debby Smith, thank you for your wisdom and for those eagle eyes of yours. I am also grateful for our friendship. To Betsy Thorpe, thank you for your assistance in the organization of this book and for your encouragement. Your guidance changed how I saw my work. Peter Muller, you made me a better writer and this a better book. Our conversations about life and love were the cherry on top. My appreciation of you is boundless.

To my California Narrative Therapy Community, especially Michael Arcuri, Delia Horwitz, Carrie Asuncion, and Marti Glenn, thank you for our explorations about love and connection.

To eleven dedicated manuscript readers: Ellen Winner, Lillah Schwartz, Diane Tower-Jones, Randy Hale, Cheryl Conner, Delia Horwitz, Shelley Glinsky, Devaya Smith, Lynn Edgar, Tracey Lilly, and Kory Garretson. Having your eyes on my words and ideas mattered. I could not have done this without you. An extra special bow to Tracey and Kory for most hours in the reading chair. My gratitude to you both for the time, energy, and commitment.

Donna Dawson, thank you for giving me reasons to speak early on, rather than remain silent and careful. You treated every student with respect. This made a profound and long-standing impression on me.

Thanks to each of you who gave me permission to write a client conversation based on one we had and include it here. You are my secret favorite humans for your willingness to contribute to others in this profound way.

To my daughter, MacKenzie, thank you for helping me remember how it is to be brand-new on this planet. Thank you for reminding me about freedom. "Love you forever, like you for always, as long as I'm living, my daughter you'll be."

Thank you, Corky Fowler, for being MacKenzie's father. Thank you for our visits many years later to unwind the moments when both of us were young and afraid. (Corky died during the writing of this book, but the conversation with him continues.)

To my partner, Eric, who passed away in 2017. Wherever you are now, darling, thank you for being my man for seventeen years. Life with you was never dull, and I learned so much being toe-to-toe. Our laughter saved us. Each time we chose silly over serious, easier over difficult, and simple over complicated, we grew closer. Thank you for loving me. I love you forever. Let's meet again someday and catch up.

REFERENCES

1 https://www.legalhandle.com/divorce-rates.html.

2 https://wernererhardquotes.wordpress.com/2010/01/22/responsibility-begins-with-the-willingness-to-take-the-stand-that-one-is-cause-in-the-matter-of-one%E2%80%99s-life-it-is-a-declaration-not-an-assertion-that-is-it-is-a-context-from-which-one-choos/

3 O'Donohue, John. *To Bless the Space between Us: A Book of Blessings.* New York: Doubleday, 2008.

4 Dispenza, Joe. *Breaking the Habit of Being Yourself: How to Lose Your Mind and Create a New One,* 22. London: Hay House, 2012.

5 Dispenza, *Breaking the Habit of Being Yourself,* 61-62.

6 https://www.ncbi.nlm.nih.gov/pmc/articles/PMC4006178/

7 Dispenza, *Breaking the Habit of Being Yourself,* 53.

8 http://www.space.com/21413-hadfield-astronaut-health-return-earth.html

9 Doidge, Norman. Essay. In *The Brain That Changes Itself: Stories of Personal Triumph from the Frontiers of Brain Science,* 15. Penguin Group, 2007.

10 https://www.jenkemmag.com/home/2019/03/20/science-behind-overcoming-fear/

11 https://www.nationalgeographic.com/adventure/article/most-dangerous-free-solo-climb-yosemite-national-park-el-capitan

12 https://www.nationalgeographic.com/adventure/features/athletes/alex-honnold/most-dangerous-free-solo-climb-yosemite-national-park-el-capitan/

13 https://www.nationalgeographic.com/adventure/features/athletes/alex-honnold/most-dangerous-free-solo-climb-yosemite-national-park-el-capitan/

14 https://www.nationalgeographic.com/adventure/features/athletes/alex-honnold/most-dangerous-free-solo-climb-yosemite-national-park-el-capitan/

15 https://www.cnn.com/2010/OPINION/03/23/brizendine.male.brain/index.html

16 Brizendine, Louann. *The Male Brain,* 2. Bantam, 2011.

17 https://www.ncbi.nlm.nih.gov/pmc/articles/PMC2763521/

18 https://www.ncbi.nlm.nih.gov/pmc/articles/PMC5087699/278

19 Darling, Haavio-Mannila & Kontula, 2001; Kontula, 2009

[20] https://www.brainyquote.com/quotes/marianne_williamson_108542

[21] https://www.rickhanson.net/how-your-brain-makes-you-easily-intimidated/

[22] Brizendine, Louann. *The Female Brain*, 97. Broadway Books, a division of Random House, Inc., New York, 2006.

[23] https://www.webmd.com/infertility-and-reproduction/news/20030626/male-biological-clock-ticking-too

[24] Center for Action and Contemplation. "Good and Bad Power," Weekly Summary Newsletter, August 8–13, 2021.

[25] https://www.azquotes.com/author/18308-Richard_Rohr/tag/pain.

[26] https://www.stress.org/stress-effects/.

[27] https://www.healthline.com/health/stress

[28] https://www.mayoclinic.org/healthy-lifestyle/stress-management/in-depth/stress-relievers/art-20047257

[29] Rūmī Jalāl al-Dīn. *The Essential Rumi: New Expanded Edition*, translated by Coleman Barks, 16. San Francisco, CA: Harper, 2004.

[30] http://www.rickhanson.net/contact/faqs/

[31] https://www.webmd.com/balance/stress-management/features/how-anger-hurts-your-heart

[32] Epstein, David. "Men Hear Women's Melodies." *Discover*, November 22, 2005. http://discovermagazine.com/2005/nov/men-hear-womens.

[33] https://www.cleveland.com/business/2016/01/why_do_70_percent_of_lottery_w.html

[34] https://images.squarespace-cdn.com/content/54b5c1d4e4b060f2e9699962/1428449932074-FIZAXT8IYVGFEODB55FM/only-make.jpg?format=2500w&content-type=image%2Fjpeg

BIBLIOGRAPHY

Anwar, Gabrielle and Catherine Oxenberg. Documentary: *Sexology*. Journeyman Pictures, 2016.

Armstrong, Alison. *Making Sense of Men: A Woman's Guide to a Lifetime of Love, Care, and Attention from All Men*. 2007.

Barks, Coleman. *The Essential Rumi*. HarperOne, 2004.

Boyle, Father Gregory. *Tattoos on the Heart*. Free Press, 2011.

Brizendine, Dr. Louann. *The Female Brain*. Broadway Books, 2006. *The Male Brain*. Broadway Books, 2010.

Coelho, Paulo. *The Alchemist*. HarperOne, 2014.

Dispenza, Dr. Joe. *Breaking the Habit of Being Yourself: How to Lose Your Mind and Create a New One*. Hay House, 2012.

Doige, Norman. *The Brain That Changes Itself*. Penguin Life, 2007.

Dubac, Robert. *Inside the Male Intellect*. Directed by Michael Drumm, 2005.

Gandhi, Dr. Arun. *The Gift of Anger: And Other Lessons from My Grandfather Mahatma Gandhi*. Gallery/Jeter Publishing, 2017.

Gay, Ross. *The Book of Delights: Essays*. Algonquin Books, 2019.

Gottman, John. *Eight Dates: Essential Conversations for a Lifetime of Love*. Workman Publishing Company, 2019.

Gungor, Mark. *Laugh Your Way to a Better Marriage*. Atria Books, 2009.

Hansen, Dr. Rick. *Resilient: How to Grow an Unshakable Core of Calm, Strength, and Happiness*. Harmony, 2018.

Harvey, Steve. *Act Like a Lady, Think Like a Man*. Amistad, 2014.

Honnold, Alex. Documentary: *Free Solo*. Directed by Elizabeth Chai Vasarhelyi, Jimmy Chin, 2018.

Katie, Byron. *A Thousand Names for Joy: Living in Harmony with the Way Things Are*. Harmony, 2008.

Kelly, Scott. *Endurance: A Year in Space, a Lifetime of Discovery.* Vintage, 2018.

O'Donohue, John. *To Bless the Space Between Us: A Book of Blessings.* Doubleday, 2008.

Oliver, Mary. *Why I Wake Early: New Poems.* Beacon Press, 2005.

Rohr, Richard. *Immortal Diamond: The Search for Our True Self.* Jossey-Bass, 2013.

Tolle, Eckhart. *The Power of Now: A Guide to Spiritual Enlightenment.* New World Library, 2004.

Twist, Lynn. *The Soul of Money: Transforming Your Relationship with Money and Life.* W. W. Norton & Company, 2017.

Wall Kimmerer, Robin. *Gathering Moss: A Natural and Cultural History of Mosses.* Oregon State University Press, 2003.

Westover, Tara. *Educated: A Memoir.* Random House, 2018.

Wilczek, Frank. *A Beautiful Question: Finding Nature's Deep Design.* Penguin Books, 2016.

Printed in the United States
by Baker & Taylor Publisher Services